Busy Moms

A Farm to Table Fabulous Cookbook

Busy Moms

A Farm to Table Fabulous Cookbook

Kimberly Storm Ritter

978-1-934817-50-6

First Edition

10 9 8 7 6 5 4 3 2 1

Great American
COOKBOOKS

a subsidiary of:

Great American Publishers
171 Lone Pine Church Road • Lena, MS 39094
TOLL-FREE 1.888.854.5954 • www.GreatAmericanPublishers.com

Kimberly Storm Ritter

Layout & Design: Nichole Stewart
Production Assistant: Zak Simmons

Contents

In Loving Memory

These amazing busy moms will continue to remain in my heart forever and will never be forgotten: my grandmas Margaret Storm, Olivia Kenosky, and Jean Kania; my aunt Nelda Storm; my stepsister Tami Kester; and my dear friend Ann Marie Demuth.

Dedication

I wouldn't even have the proper title of "Busy Mom" without my amazing Kaden. I'll never forget the moment the nurses handed me that beautiful baby with dimples. Everything about him was perfect, even his tiny fingernails. I thought, *Anyone who doubts the existence of God should be present for the birth of a child.* They would never have doubt again after seeing such a miracle. In that moment, my life changed forever. I never thought I could love another human being so much. It was a different kind of love. "Overwhelming," in a good way, is maybe the best word to describe that kind of unconditional love. It's almost like children make you feel every emotion you could ever possibly feel, all at once! They test the limits of our strength and sanity while also making us feel so fulfilled.

As a self-proclaimed career woman, I really never thought I could love anything more than my career and my family. I worked all the time. I was sending out-of-office emails to my clients while in labor. I thought that the minute I had my baby, I would be back at my computer. I mean, how could I, as a sales rep, be away from my territory that long and not be forgotten by my customers? I'd just have the baby and go right back to work without skipping a beat. Well, that thought process changed in a minute after looking into those eyes. He needed me from the moment he entered this world, and everything from that moment on was about him. I took the longest maternity leave I could without losing my job, and then it was about how quickly I could get home to my baby every single day thereafter.

I'm so grateful God trusted me with this beautiful soul named Kaden. I truly thank God for him every single day. He's smart, spirited, creative, persistent, determined, sweet, kind, thoughtful, hilarious, and surely keeps me on my toes. Before I had him, I didn't even know I had a voice like the one I have when I'm standing up for my son. I'll always fight for him, defend him when he's right, make him admit when he's wrong so he learns from his mistakes, and have his back because I am setting an example for him to be strong. Yes, I'll spoil him, buy him things I can't really afford, and smother him with love because childhood is just a fleeting moment in time. I will teach him as best I can to be courageous and kind in this world, where amongst all the beauty, more emphasis is often placed on the negativity. I hope he is always able to see the beauty in the little things like he does now.

My beautiful Kaden, I'm so proud of you, and I love you to the moon, stars, and California. To my Little Man, my KK, Kaden Robert Storm, I dedicate this book. Your busy mom will never be too busy for you!

Foreword

Beyond blessed and excited is how I feel to be sharing some of my favorite go-to recipes with all of you in this easy-to-follow cookbook for the busy family. Trying to decide what's for dinner can be just another daunting task when juggling family, career, a home, and everything else. It's overwhelming sometimes to get creative or even please everyone when you're exhausted at the end of a crazy day. An unexpected call from the school to pick up your child early, an impromptu baseball practice, a trip to the vet with a sick pet, or one of the million things that can happen at your house as a homeowner are all things to which most moms can relate. As a busy mom, writer, wife, homeowner, and all of the other hats I wear as a modern-day working mom, I struggle with the decision of what to feed my family.

For my family, food is at the center of everything we do. If we are excited about a good report card, we share a fabulous dinner to celebrate. If we've just made it through a successful market event, we go out for dinner to rejoice its completion. If it's a holiday, it is all about whatever tradition we have for dinner that really makes it extra special. Memories are made with food. Now I'm not going to lie. We don't sit around the table every single night like an '80s sitcom. I wish we had time, but some nights it's just not possible. However, when we do, I like to make it special.

My mother is a tremendous cook, and I'm fortunate to have learned everything I know from her. When I was a little girl, back in the '70s, we lived nestled between my grandparents' chicken farm and my cousins, aunts, and uncles on Storm Road. My mother was a young mom in comparison

to other families. I had the hip, cool parents. When any of my cousins had a prom or a date, they came to my mom, so she could do their makeup. My mother had long, straight, dark brown hair that cascaded down her back and many referred to her as "Cher." She really could have been the twin of the pop sensation. Oh, if I could only turn back time! My parents often played music together so it was a fit. Mom would sing and Dad played his famous blue Fender guitar. Yes, he had a mustache just like Sonny Bono, too. They played mostly at benefits and fund-raisers. However, when my dad was just a teenager he was in the opening band for the group Steppenwolf, and, oh, how he loved to tell that story.

My mom was a stay-at-home mom for a portion of my childhood but then went back to pursue her degree in nursing, graduating at the top of her class. We were so proud of her as she stepped up to accept her diploma. What an incredible role model she is for our family. Let me tell you, Busy Moms, if you think your kids aren't watching you work hard to make a nice life for your family, think again. They may not say it because they probably don't know how, but they are most definitely paying attention. Hang in there, because someday you'll get that "thank you." I know you say you don't need it, but who doesn't like a little validation every now and again? Until then, know that you're doing a fantastic job.

With two small children, a husband, a home, school, our extra-curricular activities, and a job taking care of others as a nurse working the 3:00 to 11:00 p.m. shift, my mother still managed to have a delicious homemade meal on the stove for us every single night. She never missed a field trip, a school event, church service, church event, or baseball game. I don't know how she did it. Not only did she do it, but she made it look easy. Now that I'm a busy mom, I realize it's anything but easy. My sister and I would come home after school, and there would be a main dish and at least two sides covered in tin foil on top of the stove for us to reheat. I couldn't wait to peek under that tin foil to see what was for dinner. In the summer, Mom always had a pasta salad, fruit salad, and things we could reheat in the fridge so we ate healthily. Eventually, she would work the day shift, and we would again sit down to eat as a family. One of the constants in my life was dinner at the table with my family, and Mom did it best.

It's not easy to keep a house, work, be a wife, mother, and keep kid's schedules straight. Although I can't help with your busy schedules, I can help take the guesswork out of the age-old question: What's for dinner? If you cook even three meals a week from this book, you will be a superstar and make memories for your kids of dinner with the family. I encourage you to make extra, so you can eat leftovers a couple days a week. You can also make dinner ahead of time and just reheat. I've even included some great slow-cooker recipes, air-fryer recipes, recipes that can be easily made in the instant pot, and recipes you can freeze. I understand that due to our children's activities, many of our meals are on the run but at least they'll be homemade. It may be a weeknight, you may have three different games to attend at three different ball fields, or practice at dance studios, but there is no reason why you can't be Farm to Table Fabulous any night of the week. The key to your farm-to-table success is to have a convenient farm market, grocery store, or online source for fresh meats and veggies. If you're shopping your local grocery store, it's important to shop the perimeter of the store first. It's where you will find your freshest ingredients, produce, meats, and dairy.

Together, we will stock your pantry, cabinets, and refrigerator with go-to items to have on hand for your recipes. For me, running to the store is the most daunting task of meal prep. If I have everything on hand, it's much easier to whip something up for dinner. I highly recommend that you reward yourself the day you do your grocery shopping with an easy meal. In other words, grab yourself a rotisserie chicken or subs from the deli section, and pour yourself a nice glass of wine. By the time I shop groceries, load them in the car, unload them into the kitchen, clean out the fridge to make room for my groceries, and cook a meal, I'm beyond frazzled. Knowing dinner is already prepared makes it easier.

Another way to save yourself some time and money is with an herb or vegetable garden. If you have your own garden, then you can always snip or pick herbs and veggies at the end of the season, place them in a zip-close bag, and throw them in the freezer. I know it sounds like another task, but it's much easier to maintain than a vegetable garden if you'd like to start out simple. A couple years ago, I thought it would be a great idea to have window boxes installed on my home. My farmhouse is 150 years old, so I thought it would be a cool way to give it a little update while maintaining its historical integrity. I'm also obsessed with all things English, so they were my version of the English garden since my thumb is more light-yellow than green. It turns out the window boxes have actually become a vertical garden each spring. I grow everything from fresh basil and dill to cucumbers and summer squash. The vines cascade down my house like a waterfall. It's not unusual to hear me say, "Kaden, will you go to your bedroom and grab me some cucumbers and an eggplant?" It may sound crazy, but is also rather convenient. If windows boxes aren't your thing, you can also fill a big flower pot with soil and grow an herb garden outside your front or back door. They grow almost anywhere.

My grandma and grandpa Storm were farmers, so gardening was their business, their livelihood. They always kept bins of fresh potatoes in the basement and onions in the attic. I don't know why the onions were in the attic other than it was cool, dry, and they had so many from their fall harvest it was the only place they had space. My maternal grandparents, although not farmers, also maintained an amazing garden and perfect fruit trees. We could literally sit in the middle of Grandma and Grandpa Kenosky's garden and eat a full vegetarian dinner followed by dessert in the blueberry patch. Because they canned everything, nothing ever went to waste, and they could eat fresh vegetables throughout the winter months. To me, that task is a little intimidating. Maybe I'll tackle it in my next book. For now we'll just freeze everything.

Reserving one day a week for meal prep can really start your week off on the right foot. You know, a "stay in your jammies all day and prep with a really good movie on TV or some soothing music" kinda day. A fully stocked freezer and pantry is also extremely helpful. When Kaden was really little and I was on the road every day as a sales rep, I planned out my meals weekly. Back then I was the epitome of a single and very busy working mom. Kaden never slept well, so I was always exhausted. I traveled in my car for a minimum of five hours a day and carried

fabric samples around the city the rest of the day for presentations to designers and architects. I actually loved my job, especially my customers, and there's just something about knowing that dinner is either prepped or ready in a slow cooker that takes a load off your shoulders when you're trying to focus on work. Knowing you don't have to stop at a busy grocery store on your way home from work is a good feeling. Prepping is key.

I'm including prep-ahead or quick recipes for the busy mom or dad for every day of the week. This book will make meal prep for your family super simple, and, as always, I encourage you to create your own version of my recipes that appeal to your family. Cooking should be fun and creative. My style of cooking is very casual, so I encourage you to not take it too terribly seriously and enjoy the process. As always, I encourage you make it extra special by lighting some candles to add sparkle or serving on your best china. No matter what, always make it your own version of Farm to Table Fabulous!

Thank you to my husband—my love, my rock, my best friend. I truly love you more and more each day. You've completed our family in a way I could never have imagined. You support my dreams, even though you barely have time for your own. You set a good example for Kaden every single day on how to be a kind, generous, hardworking, and loving man. You are an incredible role model. I could never have done any of this without you. I am forever grateful for you and the love we share. Just when I thought I couldn't possibly have any more love in my heart as a busy, single mom, you came along and proved me wrong. From our first dance and our 1980s-rom-com first kiss, I've loved you. Thank you for supporting us while also giving me the gift of quality time with my son while he's young enough to appreciate it. You work hard for us and never complain. Thank you for making me realize my dreams and to embrace the gifts I never even knew I had. There's only one word to describe our love and life together—magic.

To my mom and Kaden's mom-mom, you are the quintessential busy mom, even now! Thank you for supporting me always and being the ultimate role model. Thank you for showing me how to manage a career and a family. You truly know how to make a house a home and how to make a memory for your children. I owe my fondest memories to you. I'm basically taking everything I've learned from you and applying it to my life on a daily basis. If I'm even half the mom you are, then I feel like I'm doing alright. I'm very, very grateful for you and your unconditional love. I love you more!

To all the busy moms in my life who continue to help me along life's journey, I appreciate you all more than you can possibly imagine. My wonderful friends both old and new, aunts, cousins, my sister Nicole, sisters-in-law Leslie and Carol, and mother-in-law Liane, you busy moms all continue to be my village in the midst of your own crazy schedules. I love you so much and genuinely thank you. I'm truly blessed to be surrounded by such amazing women!

To my Great American Publisher's family, especially Sheila and Nichole, the busy moms with whom I'm blessed to work with every day, I thank you again for this amazing opportunity. I consider you all my family and the most incredible, inspiring group of individuals. Thank you for believing in me and for all your support. It is truly a dream to get to work with you on another wonderful project, and I love you all dearly.

Busy Mom Essentials

We must accept that the idea of dinner as the most important family meal of the day isn't going anywhere, no matter how busy our lives get. This list of Busy Mom Essentials is meant to help you cook meals for your family in the fastest, easiest way possible. With a little preparation, this list will help you provide great Farm to Table Fabulous meals for your family while leaving you with enough energy to enjoy them as well.

HERBS & SPICES:

I realize not everyone likes all of these spices, so revise this list to meet your family's needs. Fresh herbs are best, but dry herbs can almost always be substituted in a recipe. These are the herbs and spices I use the most in many of my recipes.

all-purpose seasoning

allspice (*Pimenta dioica*)

basil (*Ocimum basilicum*)

bay leaf (*Laurus nobilis*)

black pepper (*Piper nigrum*)

cayenne pepper (*Capsicum annuum*)

celery seed (*Apium graveolens*, **variety** *dulce*)

chili powder

chives (*Allium schoenoprasum*)

cilantro (*Coriandrum sativum*)

cinnamon (*Cinnamomum verum*)

clove (*Syzygium aromaticum*)

coriander (*Coriandrum sativum*)

cumin (*Cuminum cyminum*)

curry

dill (*Anethum graveolens*)

fennel (*Foeniculum vulgare*)

garlic powder

ginger (*Zingiber officinale*)

Italian seasoning

nutmeg (*Myristica fragrans*)

onion powder

oregano (*Origanum vulgare*)

paprika (*Capsicum annuum*)

parsley (*Petroselinum crispum*)

rosemary (*Rosmarinus officinalis*)

saffron (*Crocus sativus*)

sage (*Salvia officinalis*)

sea salt

sesame (*Sesamum indicum*)

tarragon (*Artemisia dracunculus*)

thyme (*Thymus vulgaris*)

turmeric (*Curcuma longa*)

vanilla (*Vanilla planifolia* **and** *V. tahitensis*)

white mustard (*Sinapis alba*)

white pepper

FRESH STAPLES:

These staples keep well in a cool, dry place and are essential to have on hand for day-to-day cooking.

ginger root	white and red potatoes
lemons	shallots
white and red onions	

PANTRY STAPLES:

If you are just getting your feet wet in the kitchen of your new home (not literally because if that's the case you may want to get your money back or call a plumber), this list is perfect for getting you started. If you are a seasoned cook, you may have most of these pantry staples on hand already. Take a deep breath. This list is only suggested items to make life a little easier, so you're not running to the store last minute. I'm not terribly organized, so it happens to me all the time. This list helps to keep me in check. You also know that I live in a farmhouse that is 150 years old, so closet and cabinet space is at a premium.

all-purpose flour	panko breadcrumbs
apple cider vinegar	plain breadcrumbs
artichoke hearts	pasta (penne, spaghetti, spirals, fettuccine, large
balsamic vinegar	shells, no-bake lasagna noodles)
beef stock	rice (white, brown, basmati, arborio)
Calamata olives	rice wine vinegar
canned beans (white kidney, Northern	roasted red peppers (unless you prefer to
white, garbanzo)	make your own)
capers	sesame oil
chicken stock	sour cream
crushed tomatoes	soy sauce
diced tomatoes	sugar
Dijon mustard	teriyaki sauce
evaporated milk	tomato paste
extra virgin olive oil (I use this in	tomato purée
almost every recipe)	truffle oil
ketchup	white vinegar
white horseradish	vegetable or canola oil for frying
Italian breadcrumbs	vegetable stock
Italian dressing	Worcestershire sauce

MEATS:

Remember, it's still farm to table and fresh, even if you purchase your fresh meats beforehand and freeze them. Just take them out the day before you plan to use them and transfer to the fridge to defrost. For a quicker defrosting, place packaged meat in cool water until defrosted or use your instant pot. It's usually cheaper to purchase meat in bulk. You can then repackage into zip-close bags in dinner portions for your family. If you go the the grocery store, farmers market, or butcher once a week, you can buy enough for the week. Therefore, keep some in the fridge that you plan to cook immediately and put the rest in the freezer. If you're planning out the month and have a chest freezer (God bless you), get it all!

Here are my suggestions of meats to have on hand in your freezer:

beef cubes	pork tenderloin
Delmonico steak	pork chops
filet mignon	pork ribs
flank steak	ground beef
pot roast	ground turkey
chicken breast	ground chicken
chicken strips	sweet sausage
chicken thighs and legs (boneless and/or bone in)	kielbasa
	fillet of salmon
whole chicken or roaster	jumbo shrimp
halibut	scallops
pork butt	tilapia

INSTANT POT IDEAS

If you happen to have an instant pot, this quick reference can really help you during the meal prep process.

1. Defrosting meat: This is a huge time saver on a busy weeknight. Pour 1 cup water into your pressure cooker. Place a trivet on the bottom, tall enough so meat doesn't touch water. Put your pound (or up to 2 pounds) on your trivet. Close lid and steam valve. Set to high pressure for 10 minutes. Do a quick release. Pour out liquid that has accumulated inside your instant pot.

2. Mashed potatoes: This is always a great side dish for just about any meal. Who doesn't love something served over mashed potatoes? Here's how to make them in minutes. Place the peeled and sliced potatoes into the bottom of the instant pot. Cover with water and add 1 teaspoon salt. Place the lid on the instant pot and set the valve to seal. Cook on manual pressure for 8 minutes. When the timer goes off, turn the instant pot off. Quick release the pressure from the pot.

3. Boiled eggs: Hard-boiled eggs are a great go-to breakfast for busy families. They also make a great snack to keep in the fridge or to add protein to any salad. Place 1 cup water in instant pot. Add egg or steam rack and carefully set as many eggs as desired on or in rack. Place lid on cooker and set cook time for 5 minutes on high pressure. Once cook time has elapsed, let pressure release for 5 minutes.

4. Roaster chicken: This is something that is so versatile. From Sunday supper and quick quesadillas to the perfect protein for a quick salad or sandwich, it's always great to have one of these cooked and in the fridge ready to go. Use 2 cups water if you have an 8-quart instant pot. Place cut lemon, onion, and fresh garlic inside cavity of chicken and place chicken on trivet in instant pot. Add salt and pepper. Place lid on cooker and be sure valve is turned to sealed. Set on high pressure for 6 minutes per pound of chicken.

5. Rice: This is another great side to accompany just about any meal. Make it ahead of time to reheat and serve throughout the week. Add 1:1 rice to water ratio into pot. Cook 3 minutes at high pressure. Natural pressure release for 11 to 18 minutes.

God could not be everywhere, therefore he made mothers. —Rudyard Kiplng

*A*h, the appetizer. It can set the tone for a beautiful dinner or be the star of the show for a memorable party. But have you considered the appetizer for a simple supper?

When I think back to some of my fondest food memories, the entire offering was simple appetizers. New Year's Eve as a child was thirty family members squeezed into my grandmother's farm-house waiting for the clock to strike midnight just so we could dig into those mini hot dogs wrapped in pastry. Otherwise known to most as pigs in a blanket, we dipped them in mustard and were my all-time favorite appetizer as a child. My son, Kaden, loves them as well. It's funny how food creates such wonderful traditions and memories. As a busy, working mom, I love to create those memories for my son any chance I get.

Making appetizers for what I like to call a "simple supper" is a great way to create memories. If you know me and my Farm-to-Table Fabulous brand, then you know I'm obsessed with nostalgia and tradition. As a busy mom, however, I love finding new traditions to celebrate with my family in addition to sharing the ones from my childhood. My hope is that this book is your go-to resource which will allow you to create your own memories and traditions even during a busy week. Appetizers are a great place to start.

Whether you're making an appetizer to tide the kids over until dinner, to greet your dinner guests or to set the tone for a special weekend meal, don't save the apps for just a holiday. Make those special memories any night of the week.

F2T Fabulous Tip: Make any night of the week a little extra special by making an appetizer to enjoy during cocktail hour (with or without alcohol.) This will allow your family to slow down and get settled in for the evening. Pick a night where nothing else is planned outside the home and celebrate just being together. Appetizers make any night special.

This is one of my favorite refreshing dips. That's a huge statement, because I love dip. This is like a taco on a chip minus the meat. My mom would put this out on taco or fajita night so we would gather in the kitchen while she was cooking. I think it also helped take the edge off our hunger while she was prepping dinner.

Cold Taco Dip

Yield: 10 to12 servings

1 cup (8 ounces) sour cream
1 (1-ounce) envelope taco seasoning
2 cups (8 ounces) shredded Cheddar cheese
1 cup chopped Vidalia onion
4 cups shredded lettuce
1½ cups chopped tomatoes
Tortilla chips

In a small mixing bowl, combine sour cream and taco seasoning until blended. Spread onto a 12-inch round serving platter or shallow bowl. Top with cheese, onion, lettuce and tomatoes. Serve with tortilla chips.

Most kids, especially tweens and teens, love pizza rolls. This is my cost-effective, healthier version. It may be even more fun than pizza. Yes, you read that right. Your kids will have fun making it and eating it, instead of just placing an order. The best part is that if your kiddos aren't necessarily fond of pepperoni, you can stuff the baguette with just about anything—mushrooms, peppers, onions, cooked sausage crumbles, beef, ham, pineapple—the possibilities are endless.

Stuffed Pepperoni Pizza Baguette

Yield: 10 to 12 servings

1 (14-inch) baguette
2 cups pepperoni slices
2 cups shredded mozzarella cheese
1 teaspoon olive oil

With a serrated knife, cut about 2 inches off 1 tip of baguette; reserve the trimmed end. Hollow out the inside leaving just an ⅛ inch of bread around the edges. (Be careful to not puncture through to the outside of the bread.) Holding the sealed bottom to keep from pushing through, stuff bread alternately with pepperoni, cheese and sauce. Repeat layers until full, using the handle of a spoon to pack the stuffing tight. When done, replace the reserved trimmed end. Wrap tightly in aluminum foil and bake 25 minutes at 375°. Remove from oven and raise temperature to 400°. Open aluminum foil and brush with oil; top with mozzarella cheese. Return to oven, uncovered, and cook until golden, 5 to 8 minutes more. Cool slightly before slicing into 1-inch slices using a serrated knife. May be made the night before and reheated.

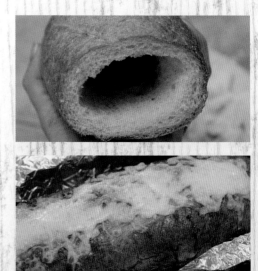

Fresh Tomato & Basil Bruschetta

Yield: 24 servings

¼ cup olive oil
3 to 4 garlic cloves, minced
4 medium tomatoes, diced
½ cup chopped fresh basil
1 loaf fresh French bread
Sea salt & pepper to taste

In a small pan over medium heat, combine oil and garlic. Sauté until translucent and fragrant. Let cool. In a bowl, add tomatoes, basil, garlic, oil and toss gently. Refrigerate at least 1 hour to allow flavors to blend. Bring to room temperature before serving. Cut bread into 24 slices; toast in 400° oven about 10 minutes or until lightly browned. Top with tomato mixture, a sprinkle of sea salt and pepper. Serve immediately.

I am a bruschetta fanatic! I love any kind of fresh, crusty bread. Add some cheese, stuffed olives and call it a meal. I really don't even need anything on top but this nice fresh bruschetta has all the best elements of a summer garden. It's light, fragrant, and delicious. This may also be made a day or two ahead of time and kept in the fridge to eat later!

Pizza 3-Ways

Yield: 1 serving

3 tablespoons pizza sauce
1 English muffin (or tortilla shell or pita)
½ cup shredded mozzarella cheese (or Feta or shredded Cheddar)

Additional Toppings:
¼ cup sliced pepperoni
Sliced mushrooms
Cooked shrimp
Chopped onion
Sliced bell peppers
Cooked sausage
Spinach
Artichoke hearts
Sliced olives
Ham
Pineapple

Preheat oven to 400°. Spread pizza sauce over English muffin sprinkle with cheese. Add toppings of your choice, if desired. Bake 10 to 12 minutes or until crispy.

Pizza is almost always a winner for the kiddos. When I was little, Grandma Storm would put sauce and cheese on a slice of bread for a quick homemade pizza. Here's an updated, tastier version using ingredients you probably have on hand. I'll give you the basic ingredients, but you can put anything you like on these tasty little treats. They're very easy to make and there's no better way to spend a night with the kiddos than creating something fun in the kitchen.

My grandma made deviled eggs for every occasion. They are one of my favorites and can be made pretty quickly once your eggs are boiled. In this recipe, we start with the basic recipe. Adding truffle oil makes an old standby appetizer just a little more sophisticated for your special occasion. Top with crispy prosciutto or dill and you're a superstar. Kids love piping the filling so it's a great way for them to have fun in the kitchen.

Perfect Deviled Eggs

Yield: 1 dozen

6 hard-boiled large eggs
½ cup mayonnaise
½ tablespoon Dijon mustard
1 tablespoon finely chopped onion
Sea salt and pepper to taste

Cut eggs in half lengthwise. Remove yolks to a zip-close plastic bag; set aside egg whites. To bag, add mayonnaise, mustard, salt and pepper; mix well. Trim corner and pipe into egg whites. Refrigerate until serving.

For Superstar Deviled Eggs, add truffle oil to taste to egg yolks before mixing. And/or cut 3 prosciutto slices into strips and bake at 400° for 15 minutes or until crispy; place on top of finished eggs. Top with 12 fresh dill sprigs.

I would like to try to make this more farm to table but why mess with perfection? This is fun for the kiddos to help make and equally fun to eat. It was a staple at Grandma Storm's family New Year's Eve party. Picture thirty people in a farmhouse in the country, the kids playing in the living room, the adults playing cards in the dining room, in a house bursting with love and laughter. That's exactly what this recipe reminds me of every time I make it.

Minidogs in a Blanket

Yield: 4 to 6 servings

1 (8-ounce) tube refrigerated crescent rolls
6 beef hot dogs (preferably no nitrates, organic)

Preheat oven to 400°. Unroll crescent dough on a cutting board or wax paper keeping it in 1 piece. Cut strips that are almost as wide as the hot dogs. Cut hot dogs in half lengthwise. Roll each half in dough until fully covered; cut dough. Pinch dough with fingertips to seal. Place on an ungreased baking sheet. Repeat until all hot dogs are rolled in dough. Bake 15 minutes or until golden brown. Remove from oven, transfer to cutting board and slice into bite-size pieces. Serve with ketchup or mustard for dipping.

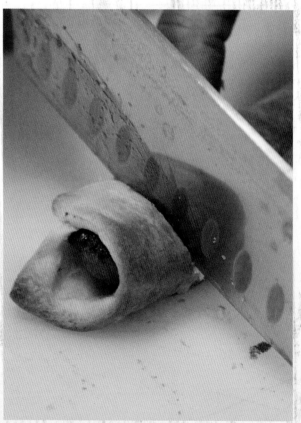

Ham & Cheese Roll Up

1 (8-ounce) tube refrigerated crescent rolls
6 slices honey ham
6 slices sharp American cheese
1 cup shredded Cheddar cheese

Unroll dough in 1 piece. Line with a layer of ham, then American cheese and finish with Cheddar cheese. Roll up tightly and slice into 1- to 2-inch slices. Lay flat on a baking sheet coated with cooking spray. Bake at 375° for 15 to 20 minutes.

This is a fun twist on the ham and cheese sandwich. It's ready in a snap and is a hot meal instead of a cold sandwich. They are just as good cold, though, so if you happen to have leftovers, send them with your kiddos for lunch the following day. They will be the superstar of the lunch room.

I love making this recipe to utilize my leftover chicken. If you're preparing these in the summertime or even in a hot kitchen, keep them separated on a floured surface. I cannot stress this enough or you will end up with a big ball of dough. They will also break apart during cooking if you do not seal them properly. We made these for one of our Farm-to-Table Dinners at the market and that's exactly what happened. Talk about a rookie mistake. Yes. Even the so-called professionals mess up every now and again, so give yourself a break. You may also make this ahead of time and freeze. Kids love these Chicken Dumplings because they're small, tasty, and fun for dipping.

Chicken Dumplings

Yield: 4 dozen

1 pound cooked chicken breast, cut into chunks
1½ cups sliced fresh mushrooms
1 small onion, cut into wedges
½ green cabbage
2 to 3 tablespoons soy sauce plus more for dipping
1 (14-ounce) package potsticker dumpling wrappers

In a food processor, combine chicken, mushrooms, onion, cabbage and soy sauce. Process until blended. Bring a pot of water to a boil while preparing dumplings. Place 1 tablespoon chicken mixture in the center of each wrapper. (Until ready to use, keep wrappers covered with a damp towel to prevent them from drying out.) Moisten edges with water. Bring opposite sides together to form a triangle; pinch to seal. Working in batches, drop dumplings in boiling water; cook 3 to 4 minutes or until they float. Serve dumplings with soy sauce for dipping. Refrigerate leftovers.

Optional: Dumpling Lasagna. Treat an 8x8-inch baking dish with sesame oil. Make a single layer of 9 dumpling wrappers; spread evenly with meat mixture. Repeat 2 more times to create "lasagna." In a bowl, combine ½ tablespoon soy sauce and 1 tablespoon honey. Pour over top layer. Bake, covered, 20 minutes and uncovered an additional 10 minutes.

Cheesy Quesadillas

Yield: 4 servings

4 (9-inch) flour tortillas
2 cups shredded Mexican cheese blend
2 tablespoons butter
¼ teaspoon chili powder
¼ teaspoon onion powder
Salt and pepper
½ cup sour cream
½ cup salsa

Place 2 tortillas on a baking sheet. Spread 1 cup cheese over each tortilla. Place second tortilla on top. In a small pot over low heat, melt butter with chili powder, onion powder, salt and pepper. Brush over both sides of each tortilla. Broil approximately 4 inches from heat 1 to 2 minutes each side or until golden brown. Watch very closely. Cut into wedges. Combine sour cream and salsa to serve for dipping.

Kids not only enjoy eating these, but love helping make them too. Add meat and your cheesy quesadilla just became a very filling main dish. You can whip these up in minutes for an easy weeknight meal, and it's a very easy recipe to double or even triple if you're really hungry.

This recipe says holiday to me. Anytime I'm stuffing something, anything, it feels a little extra special and decadent. These are easy to just pop in your mouth, so plan accordingly if you have people with big appetites. In other words, maybe double this one. It's also hearty enough for a simple supper paired with a salad.

Sausage-Stuffed Mushrooms

Yield: 2 dozen

1 pound sweet Italian sausage, casings removed
24 ounces (approximately 24) medium to large baby bella mushrooms
1 celery stalk, finely chopped
2 tablespoons onion, finely chopped
2 garlic cloves, minced
2 tablespoons minced fresh parsley
½ cup panko breadcrumbs
¾ cup grated Parmesan cheese, divided
Salt and pepper to taste

In a skillet, brown sausage until fully cooked and no longer pink, about 8 to 10 minutes. Remove stems from mushrooms and set caps aside. Chop stems and add to skillet along with celery; cook 3 to 4 minutes. In a bowl, combine onion, garlic, parsley and breadcrumbs. Stir in ½ cup Parmesan and sausage mixture. Spoon 1 to 2 teaspoons sausage mixture into each cap. Place on a large baking sheet coated with cooking spray. Sprinkle with remaining ¼ cup Parmesan. Bake at 350° for 15 to 20 minutes or until mushrooms are tender and filling is lightly browned. Serve warm.

Macaroni & Cheese Ham Cups

Yield: 4 servings

½ (16-ounce) box campanelle pasta
2 cups whole milk
2 tablespoons butter
1 cup sharp American cheese
1 cup sharp Cheddar cheese
Salt and pepper
12 slices honey ham

Place pasta in boiling water and cook until tender, about 10 minutes. Drain and place in a bowl. Cook milk and butter over low heat until butter melts. Slowly add cheeses and stir until completely melted. Pour cheese sauce over pasta. Mix with spoon until blended. Season to taste with salt and pepper. Preheat oven to 400°. Line a 12-hole cupcake tin with ham ensuring each hole is lined completely and ham hangs over slightly. Spoon pasta and sauce into ham cups. Bake 30 minutes. Remove cups from tin and serve warm.

What's a cookbook without macaroni and cheese? If your kiddos are super picky eaters, you can always replace the campanelle pasta with elbow macaroni. I say whatever it takes to get them to eat at dinnertime. I can't resist sharing this recipe because it's so darn cute and equally delicious. It's a complete meal that is super fun to eat.

Fry anything and I am 100 percent in. I mean, Oreos are a little questionable, but I've never tried them so I'm not ruling them out. It makes it very difficult to stay slim, but they say, "no one trusts a skinny cook," right? I believe in everything in moderation. You can absolutely eat fried foods as long as it's not every day. This is a great special occasion app and perfect when you can just grab the vegetables from your garden. Pile them high like pancakes, drizzle with sauce, and serve with a salad for a simple supper. Be warned, these Zucchini Fritters are so good they may be swiped right from the paper towel, never making it to the plate.

Zucchini Fritters

Yield: 1 dozen

1 large zucchini, shredded (about 3 cups)
3 tablespoons finely chopped scallions
1 egg
1 cup flour
1 teaspoon baking powder
2 tablespoons sun-dried tomato
1 cup shredded mozzarella cheese
Vegetable oil for frying, about ½ cup
½ teaspoon salt
¼ teaspoon pepper
Marinara sauce for dipping

Squeeze moisture out of shredded zucchini with paper towels. Place in a bowl and combine with scallions, egg, flour, baking powder, tomato and cheese. Heat vegetable oil in a large skillet over medium heat. Working in batches, drop tablespoonfuls of the mixture into hot oil. Fry approximately 4 minutes per side. Flatten with your spatula after flipping the first time. Lay on paper towels to drain. Sprinkle with salt and pepper. Serve with marinara sauce.

Breaded Ranch Zucchini Chips

Yield: 4 servings

2 small zucchini, thinly sliced
2 tablespoons ranch dressing
1 cup plain breadcrumbs

In a shallow bowl, toss zucchini with ranch dressing until evenly coated. Place breadcrumbs in a zip-close plastic bag; add zucchini and shake to coat. Cook in an air fryer at 370° for 20 minutes or until desired crispness. Serve with ketchup or marinara sauce for dipping.

Trying to sneak veggies into the kiddos' diet? Masquerade them as chips and add some ranch dressing. Don't get me wrong, I'm not underestimating your child's intelligence. They'll be onto you for sure. However, these zucchini chips taste so good they're not likely to question the motive.

This combination of ingredients is heaven. It's a great way to get your kids to eat their veggies. They won't even know they're eating their spinach when it's smothered in cheese. I love the idea of something to put out before dinner every once in a while. It makes the night more of an experience, and gives me a little extra time to enjoy cooking instead of every night being super quick. This dip is perfect because it is refreshing, light, and delicious.

Spinach & Artichoke Dip

Yield: 4 cups

½ cup shredded mozzarella cheese
1 (8-ounce) package cream cheese, softened
½ cup grated Parmesan cheese
1 cup drained and roughly chopped marinated artichoke hearts
2 tablespoons plain yogurt
1 tablespoon chopped, seeded jalapeño pepper
2 cups roughly chopped fresh spinach
1 teaspoon onion powder
Salt and pepper to taste
Assorted crackers

In a bowl, combine all dip ingredients. Serve with crackers.

Warm Shrimp Dip

Yield: 4 cups

½ cup shredded mozzarella cheese
½ cup grated Parmesan cheese
½ cup spaghetti or tomato sauce
1 (8-ounce) package cream cheese, softened
2 cups deveined and roughly
chopped shrimp
3 to 4 garlic cloves, finely chopped
1 tablespoon dried parsley
Assorted crackers or fresh Italian bread

Preheat oven to 400°. In a bowl, combine all ingredients except crackers. Pour into an 8x8-inch baking dish. Bake uncovered 20 to 30 minutes until bubbly. Spread over crackers or bread.

It doesn't get any better than seafood and cream cheese. Yum! This is a rich and decadent appetizer that is super simple (which is the best part). When I was little, my mom would make the most delicious shrimp scampi in red sauce. This dip reminds me of that dinner. Serve on bread for a heartier dish and with a side salad for a simple supper.

To me, this is the superstar of all appetizers. Fortunately, my family feels the same way. This is really all you need for a complete meal. If it's Mexican night, this is the perfect introduction to your main dish.

Loaded Nachos

Yield: 4 to 6

1 pound ground beef
1 (1-ounce) envelope taco seasoning
1 (15-ounce) can black beans, drained
1 (11-ounce) bag tortilla chips
2 cups salsa
1½ cups finely shredded Cheddar cheese
2 cups shredded lettuce
1 large tomato, chopped
1 (2.25-ounce) can sliced ripe olives, drained
1 cup chopped onion
1 cup sliced jalapeños
¼ cup sour cream
1 avocado, chopped
1 fresh lime, cut into wedges
for garnish (optional)

Preheat oven to 400°. In a skillet, cook meat. Add taco seasoning and mix. Add beans to warm. On a baking sheet, place an even layer of tortilla chips. Spread meat over tortilla chips, cover with salsa and top with cheese. Bake until cheese is melted. Remove from oven and top with lettuce, tomato, olives, onion and peppers. Top with sour cream and avocado and serve from baking sheet. Garnish with lime wedges if desired.

Local · NO Pesticides!
Yellow & Green
Beans
$2.99 lb.

Kirby
2 for $1.

— Local —
Kirby
Cukes
$1.99 lb.

Local
Cucumbers
$1.00 each

Vine Ripe
Tomatoes

Fo
Produce

Fresh Food

Tomatoes
$1.99 lb.

I live for a good salad. With the right protein, it really is a complete and satisfying meal. When eating out for dinner, I love to indulge in appetizers and dessert, so I often opt for a salad because it's a nice light yet filling meal. Special moments from my childhood, when the whole family was invited to our house, always included my mom's top three specialty party salads—potato salad, macaroni salad, and coleslaw. Coleslaw also accompanies our lobster tails on Christmas Eve. Need I say more?

Salad dressings almost deserve their own chapter as they have become one of my obsessions. Store-bought dressing is an option only when I'm really short on time. It's so easy to whip up your own dressing if you have a little extra time and so well worth it. They also keep well in the fridge and are very cost effective. If you have nothing on hand with no time to run to the store, extra virgin olive Oil with a splash of balsamic vinegar or fresh squeeze of lemon juice makes a quick salad dressing that is both healthy and delicious because it truly enhances the taste of the fresh vegetables in your salad.

Because I grew up in a family that sold produce in a stand alongside our Pennsylvania roads, I truly appreciate the hard work that goes into everything grown for our table. Of course, now I'm married to a farmer so that appreciation goes even deeper. I always say that just because something isn't deemed "local" doesn't mean that a farmer somewhere didn't work really hard to be certain that vegetable was cared for and picked at just the right time for your table. Farmers work from dawn to dusk in their fields. They often miss family occasions and holidays because their work day never ends. Don't forget to thank a farmer. After all, they make farm to table possible for us all.

Salads encompass everything that's seasonal and beautiful in a garden. The more color, the better. Because people eat first with their eyes, this is the perfect opportunity to knock their socks off with color.

 F2T Fabulous Tip: Take a trip to your garden, local farmers market or produce section of your grocery store with your children to let them pick out their favorite items for a salad. Take home your treasures for a salad night. You make the protein and let the kids help make their salads. Serve the masterpieces on your vintage china, wedding china or dinner plates to make it a little extra special. After all, you wouldn't frame a beautiful piece of art with Styrofoam. Take it a step further by snapping a pic for Pinterest, Facebook, Instagram or frame it for your home. I love food photography and I also love sharing my ideas with other families to enjoy.

This is the first, in the top three, go-to summer salads of my childhood and today. It is the absolute best potato salad I have ever tasted. Of course, my mother is a culinary genius so, duh! When I was a kid, the potato salad was made with my grandma Kenosky's famous pickles, so it was extra special. Today, I still think the pickles and pickle juice are the best not-so-secret ingredients ever. This recipe was made for every fond memory of a summer get-together I had growing up, and now I make it for our markets for everyone to enjoy. The longer it sits in the fridge, the better, and the color is spectacular. The red potatoes, the light green celery, the dark green pickles, and the deep yellow egg yolks, all against the creamy white mayo, it's like a work of art.

Mom's Potato Salad

Yield: 8 to 12 servings

3 to 3½ pounds red potatoes
(about 10 medium)
8 large eggs, hard-boiled
1 medium onion, finely chopped
6 celery stalks, chopped
6 whole dill pickles, chopped
1 cup mayonnaise
¼ cup dill pickle juice
Salt and pepper to taste

In a large pot, cook whole potatoes in boiling salted water until tender but not mushy when pierced with a fork. Drain and cool. Chop potatoes into bit-sized chunks. Peel eggs; cut in half then into slices. In a bowl, place potatoes, eggs, onion, celery and pickles. Stir in mayonnaise, pickle juice, salt and pepper until mixed well. Adjust seasonings or add additional pickle juice, if necessary. Chill before serving.

Mom's Coleslaw Salad

Yield: 6 to 8 servings

1 small head cabbage, shredded
3 carrots, shredded
1 green bell pepper, chopped
¾ cup mayonnaise
¼ cup evaporated milk
½ lemon, juiced
Salt and pepper to taste

Place cabbage, carrots and pepper in a large bowl. In a small bowl, stir together mayonnaise, milk and lemon juice until blended. Pour over coleslaw, add salt and pepper and toss to coat. Refrigerate until serving.

You can't talk about summer salads without including coleslaw. Whether you're eating it as a side dish or topping your favorite sandwich, this is delicious and, you guessed it, number two on favorite summer salads. This also works beautifully with any casual seafood dish such as my fish nuggets or fried oysters. As a matter of fact, I wouldn't eat either of those without it. Fun fact, we also make this on Christmas Eve with baked lobster tail and French fries. Don't ask me why, it was the way my grandmother always made Christmas Eve dinner and now, so do I.

My mother's nostalgic recipes do not disappoint, and this one is no exception. It is number three of my top three salads. The not-so-secret ingredient in this one is olives and olive juice. The olives break down the mayo in such a way that it almost makes this salad light instead of heavy like most salads made with mayonnaise. The carrots give it a little extra crunch and color for the perfect macaroni salad for any party or barbecue. Keep this one in the fridge for a quick side any night of the week.

Mom's Macaroni Salad

Yield: 8 servings

1 (16-ounce) package elbow macaroni
1 cup mayonnaise
1 (5.75-ounce) jar sliced green olives
3 medium carrots, shredded
Salt and pepper to taste

Cook macaroni according to package directions; drain and rinse with cold water. Cool completely. Combine all ingredients, using olives and their juice, in a bowl and toss until evenly coated with mayonnaise.

Summer Peach & Tomato Salad

1 pint grape or cherry tomatoes, halved
3 tomatoes, halved then thinly sliced into wedges
6 peaches, sliced
½ red onion, thinly sliced
½ cup chopped walnuts
¼ cup blackberry vinaigrette (or balsamic vinaigrette)

In a large salad bowl, combine all ingredients except vinaigrette. About 30 minutes before serving, drizzle with vinaigrette and toss to coat.

This salad is such a huge hit in our markets. However, unless they've tried it before or fully trust me, people usually want a taste test. The flavors sound so unusual that it can be a hard sell, but it just works. We make it only in the summertime when peaches and tomatoes are at their absolute freshest. Give it a try. And bring it to a party. I promise this salad will be a huge culinary hit.

I love the idea of fresh, in-season watermelon in a salad. However, this recipe takes it to another level. It combines savory and sweet for just the right balance of flavors. It's unusual so be prepared to "sell it" to your guests. Once they try it, they will be pleasantly surprised and ask you for the recipe. Because the main ingredient is beans, it's also a very hearty salad and the perfect side dish for any simple grilled meat or fish.

Garbanzo Bean, Feta & Watermelon Salad

Yield: 4 servings

½ small watermelon
2 (15-ounce) cans garbanzo beans
(chickpeas), rinsed and drained
1 cup feta cheese
4 tablespoons vegetable oil
1 teaspoon honey
2 tablespoons balsamic vinegar

Scoop out and chop watermelon meat into small cubes; measure out 4 cups. Reserve empty shell for serving the salad. In a bowl, combine garbanzo beans, watermelon and feta. In a small bowl, whisk oil, honey and vinegar. Pour over salad and toss. Pour into hollowed shell and chill until serving.

Ritter's Sweet Corn Salad

5 ears Ritter's sweet corn, shucked
2 cups cherry tomatoes
½ cup diced red onion (1 small onion)
3 tablespoons olive oil
3 tablespoons cider vinegar
Salt and pepper to taste
½ cup fresh basil

Place corn in pot of boiling water for 3 minutes. Remove to a bowl of ice water to immediately stop the cooking. Cut kernels off the corn cobs and place in a bowl. Toss in tomatoes, onion, olive oil and vinegar. Season with salt and pepper. Add fresh basil just before serving.

This salad was an inevitable creation in our market. I mean you can't be a farm market with the absolute best sweet corn in the state of Pennsylvania and not have an equally amazing corn salad. It's seasonal which makes it extra special. This salad is simple enough to allow the natural sweet corn flavor to come through in each bite. The other fresh ingredients are just the thing to compliment it beautifully.

What's a cookbook without pasta salad? Everyone has their own version, but this one is a winner. It's light, fresh, and pretty. When asked to bring a dish to a summer party, this one is quick and easy, even last minute. In addition, you most likely have all the ingredients on hand. It is so easy to throw it in some Tupperware and away you go. My mother always kept this in the fridge in the summertime because, as a working mom, she made sure meals were covered for her children. It also doubles as a great side for dinner. Kaden has requested it be in the fridge at all times, so he has a snack when he comes home from school. It's perfect year-round.

Fresh Pasta Salad

Yield: 4 to 6 servings

2 pounds tricolor spiral pasta
1 small head broccoli, broken into pieces
½ head cauliflower, broken into pieces
1 cup coarsely chopped cucumber
2 cups cherry tomatoes, quartered
½ cup chopped red onion
1 cup grated Parmesan cheese
2 cups Italian salad dressing (I prefer Ken's Steak House Italian)
Salt and pepper to taste

Cook pasta according to package directions; drain and rinse in cold water. In a large bowl, combine pasta and vegetables. Add cheese, salad dressing, salt and pepper; toss to coat. Cover and refrigerate until serving.

With the right dressing, Caesar salad is one of my favorite salads. Add grilled chicken, and it's a complete meal. I'm thinking a beautiful outdoor picnic lunch. The chicken can be made ahead of time, as well as the dressing. Seal your washed lettuce and baked croutons in separate freezer bags. Busy moms, there is absolutely nothing wrong with picking up a bottle of your favorite Caesar dressing to cut down on prep time.

Grilled Chicken Caesar Salad

Yield 4 to 6 servings

2 boneless chicken breasts, halved
2 bunches Boston or Bibb Lettuce
8 slices Texas toast or thick white bread
2 tablespoons olive oil
Sea salt and pepper to taste

Dressing:

2 small garlic cloves, minced
1 teaspoon anchovy paste
2 tablespoons freshly squeezed lemon juice
1 teaspoon Dijon mustard
1 teaspoon Worcestershire sauce
1 cup mayonnaise
½ cup freshly grated Parmigiano-Reggiano cheese
Salt and pepper to taste

In a grill pan, cook chicken until no longer pink and internal temp reaches 165°. Cut into strips and set aside. Stack bread and cut into bite-size squares. On a pan, toss bread with olive oil, salt and pepper. Arrange on baking sheet in single layer and bake at 400° about 15 minutes or until golden brown. Let cool. In a small bowl, whisk all Dressing ingredients together until well blended. In a serving bowl, toss lettuce with dressing until evenly coated. Garnish with croutons and chicken. Serve immediately.

Classic Mediterranean Salad

Yield: 4 to 6 servings

Salad:

3 cups chopped romaine lettuce
(or mixed greens)
1 medium cucumber, sliced
1 cup crumbled feta cheese
1 cup quartered cherry tomatoes
1 small red onion, thinly sliced
½ cup pitted, halved kalamata olives

Dressing:

2 tablespoons olive oil
1 lemon, juiced
1 teaspoon dried oregano
Salt and pepper to taste

In a large salad bowl, combine all Salad ingredients. Drizzle olive oil and lemon juice over salad, sprinkle with oregano, salt and pepper; toss to coat. Serve immediately.

This Mediterranean-inspired salad combines some of my favorite flavors and is a wonderful option if you're looking for something a bit different. Add grilled lamb or another protein for a complete meal.

Asparagus & Tomato Salad

Yield: 4 to 6 servings

2 bunches asparagus
1 large tomato, chopped
½ small red onion, finely chopped
1 fresh garlic clove, minced (optional)
1 cup grated Parmesan cheese
2 tablespoons extra virgin olive oil
2 tablespoons balsamic vinegar
Coarse sea salt and pepper

Blanch asparagus by dropping into boiling water for 4 minutes. Remove immediately and submerge in bowl of ice water. Once cooled completely, dry and chopped into 1-inch pieces. Place asparagus, tomato, onion and garlic in a serving bowl. Add cheese, oil and vinegar. Toss until evenly coated. Salt and pepper to taste.

I know it can be difficult to get your kiddos to eat their veggies, but this recipe is sure to please. It's colorful, full of flavor and a delicious twist on asparagus. This combination is unique enough to be a little fancy for a party dish while keeping things cool and easy in the kitchen. It's perfect alongside steaks from the grill on a warm summer day.

We don't get many hot days here in the Northeast, but when we do, no one feels like cooking. Believe it or not, we feel like eating even less. It's on those days that a salad is the perfect supper. I like to combine a refreshing fruit with my greens on a hot day, along with a very simple dressing. Shrimp make it a complete meal that is light and a little extra special.

Kale & Watermelon Salad with Shrimp

Yield: 4 to 6 servings

2 tablespoons extra virgin olive oil
3 cups kale, stems removed
2 cups cubed watermelon
2 tablespoons feta cheese crumbles
12 large shrimp, cooked, peeled and cooled
1 avocado, diced
½ lemon, juiced
Coarse sea salt and pepper

In a bowl, massage olive oil into kale with fingers to tenderize each leaf. Add watermelon, cheese, shrimp and avocado; toss to combine. Add lemon juice; mix. Sprinkle with salt and pepper to taste.

Butterhead Lettuce & Pear Salad

Yield: 4 servings

4 cups butterhead lettuce, washed
and torn into pieces
2 cups sliced pears, Anjou or Concorde
2 tablespoons goat cheese crumbles
1 cup dried cranberries
1 cup chopped pecans
2 tablespoons extra virgin olive oil
2 tablespoons balsamic vinegar
1 tablespoon honey
½ lemon, juiced
Coarse sea salt and pepper to taste

In a bowl, place lettuce, pear, cheese, cranberries and pecans. In a separate bowl, whisk oil, vinegar, honey and lemon juice. Pour over salad and toss to coat. Add salt and pepper. Enjoy!

This salad is both refreshing and hearty. The combination of sweet and savory is the perfect balance. Add a protein such as; salmon, grilled chicken or steak to complete this meal. Don't forget a fresh loaf of bread on the side!

A mother's arms are more comforting than anyone else's. —Princess Diana

$\mathcal{S}$oup has always intimidated me, in terms of making it from scratch. I know it sounds crazy. I just never knew where to begin. Do I throw a bunch of stock in a pot with handfuls of veggies and meat? Should I put raw chicken in water and make my own stock? Honestly, I hadn't a clue. When I wanted soup, I popped open a can. I grew up surrounded by women who made some of the best soups I've ever tasted. I just never felt confident enough to try making my own, and it was always a nice treat to get homemade soup from my mom. It was one of those things when if you had a cold, mom made chicken soup. If you had a bad day, soup. A snow storm on the way? You guessed it, soup. It really does warm your heart and soul.

Soup is also the best medicine because you can throw in everything that is good and healing. If Kaden tells me his throat is sore or he's feeling under the weather, it's the first thing I cook. There's nothing like a hot soup with lots of veggies and loads of garlic to heal whatever is ailing you. Back in the day, it was soup and crackers on a TV tray along with ginger ale and cartoons on a sick day from school. It wasn't until we started our five-course farm-to-table dinners at the market that I gained confidence in the soup department. It's pretty tough to have a five-course dinner without soup. What I learned is THEY'RE ACTUALLY EASY TO MAKE! Not to mention, you can make it ahead of time and heat up individual bowls all week long. It's really perfect for the busy mom. Now that I feel like I've got a firm grip on making really great soups and stews, I'm excited to share an entire chapter's worth of these super simple and delicious recipes.

Here in the Northeast, soup is also a necessity in the winter months. It doesn't often get too hot here. The evenings, even in the middle of summer, always cool off. Therefore, soup or stew is one of those things we eat all year long. I suggest utilizing weekends for making soup. Not because they're difficult to make, but weekends usually afford more time to let the soup simmer. I personally love the feeling of a big pot of soup on the stove or a hearty stew in the slow cooker on a day I have nothing else to do. Those days don't come along often so when they do, it's nice to take full advantage by making something you can smell cooking all day long.

F2T Fabulous Tip: Make your night a little more fabulous by lighting candles with dinner. Maybe light a fire or turn on the gas or electric fireplace. Just like soup, there's something about a warm flame that makes any night a little cozier and extra special.

As a little girl, I ate many variations of this recipe. Both grandmothers and my mom made it quite often. It's a healthy soup that is high in protein. So much amazing flavor is packed into those little lentils that you'll love every bite. It's so hearty that you only need a fresh loaf of Italian or French bread to complete the meal.

Lentil Soup

Yield: 6 servings

2 cups chopped carrots
1 small onion, chopped
1 cup dried lentils, rinsed
2 garlic cloves, minced
1 teaspoon celery seed
Salt and pepper
6 cups vegetable stock
1 (28-ounce) can crushed tomatoes, undrained

Place all ingredients in a slow cooker. Cook, covered, until lentils are tender, about 4 hours on high or 8 hours on low.

Chicken & Rice Soup

1 tablespoon olive oil
1 small onion, chopped
4 to 6 celery stalks, chopped
4 to 6 carrots, chopped
6 garlic cloves, minced
1 bay leaf
Salt and pepper to taste
1 tablespoon Italian seasoning (oregano, thyme, basil, rosemary, sage)
1 pound chicken breast or rotisserie chicken, cut in large chunks
6 cups chicken stock
Dill to taste
1 cup cooked jasmine rice

Heat oil in a large pot over medium-high heat. Add onion, celery, carrots, garlic, bay leaf and seasonings; cook until onions are translucent. If using raw chicken breast, add chopped chicken and brown. (If using rotisserie chicken, it will be added later.) Add stock. Bring to a boil. Reduce heat; cover and simmer 15 minutes or until vegetables are tender. If using rotisserie chicken, add it to pot and cook until warm. Stir in dill and rice.

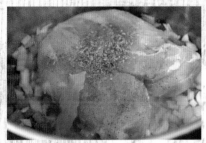

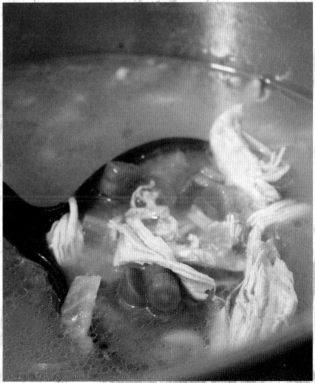

Because Kaden would eat 1,000 cans of Campbell's chicken and rice a day, I had to start making it homemade. Of course, I swiped my mom's recipe. Why reinvent the wheel? Kayden absolutely loves when mom-mom has a big pot of Chicken & Rice Soup on the stove during a sleepover. I know that when he's grown, it will be a very special memory for him. Also, this is the best medicine around during cold and flu season.

Ian's dad, my father-in-law, is an excellent cook—when he's not in the fields. He makes this soup at least once a year and it's one of my favorites. We first have it all together at a big family dinner with warm biscuits. Then he sends us home with enough for an army. Like most soups, it's even more delicious the next day. This soup is the definition of family.

Split Pea with Ham Soup

Yield: 12 servings

1 tablespoon olive oil
1 small onion, chopped
4 celery stalks, chopped
3 garlic cloves, minced
6 medium carrots, sliced
2½ pounds cooked ham
6 to 8 cups vegetable stock
Salt and pepper to taste
2 (16-ounce) bags dried green split peas

Heat oil in a stockpot over medium heat. Sauté onion, celery, garlic and carrots until fragrant. Cut ham into chunks and add to pot. Add 6 cups water, stock, salt, pepper, and peas. Cover and cook until peas are tender, about 60 minutes. Add more water if you prefer a thinner soup.

Hearty Beef Stew

Yield: 8 servings

2 to 3 pounds lean beef stew
meat, 1-inch cubes
1 tablespoon olive oil
8 medium potatoes, cubed
12 medium carrots, sliced
4 celery stalks, chopped
2 garlic cloves, minced
1 bay leaf
4 cups beef stock
1 (15-ounce) can crushed
fire-roasted tomatoes
Salt and pepper to taste
½ cup all-purpose flour
1 (8-ounce) bag frozen peas

Brown meat in oil; drain and add to slow cooker. Add potatoes, carrots, celery, garlic, bay leaf, beef stock, tomatoes, salt and pepper. Cover and cook on low 8 hours (or 4 hours on high). Whisk flour into 1 cup water until smooth; stir into stew an hour before serving. Add frozen peas, cover and cook an additional 15 minutes. Discard bay leaf.

This is one of my favorite one-pot, go-to meals, especially in the winter. The trick is to allow the beef time to cook so that it's super tender. Serve with a salad and crusty Italian bread for a complete meal.

This recipe is a wonderful option for those of you who don't eat red meat. It is still just as easy and just as delicious. Serve with cornbread, rice, a salad, or alone for a healthy, scrumptious, one-dish meal. The nice thing about chili is it can be made quickly on the stove-top or cooked all day in the slow cooker, whichever works for your schedule. Either way, it's great for a family on the go.

Turkey Chili with White Beans

Yield: 12 servings

1 small red bell pepper, chopped
1 small green bell pepper, chopped
1 medium onion, chopped
2 tablespoons olive oil
1½ pounds lean ground turkey
1½ teaspoons paprika
1½ teaspoons ground cumin
1 (15-ounce) can diced fire-roasted tomatoes, undrained
2 cups ketchup
1 tablespoon chili powder
Pinch cayenne pepper
1 teaspoon salt
1 (15-ounce) can white kidney beans
(cannellini), rinsed and drained

In a large pot, sauté peppers and onion in oil over medium heat. Add turkey and cook until meat is no longer pink; drain. Add paprika and cumin; stir and cook 1 minute longer. Stir in tomatoes, ketchup, chili powder, cayenne and salt. Bring to a boil. Reduce heat, cover and simmer 45 minutes. Add beans and heat through.

White Chicken Chili

1 pound ground chicken
1 small onion, chopped
1 tablespoon olive oil
4 garlic cloves, minced
2 (14-ounce) cans chicken broth
1 (4-ounce) can chopped jalapeños
2 teaspoons ground cumin
2 teaspoons dried oregano
1½ teaspoons cayenne pepper
1 (15-ounce) can white kidney beans
(cannellini), drained
1 (15-ounce) can garbanzo beans, drained
1 cup shredded Cheddar cheese for garnish

In a pot over medium heat, cook chicken and onion in oil until lightly browned. Add garlic; cook 1 minute longer. Stir in broth, jalapeños, cumin, oregano and cayenne; bring to a boil. Reduce heat to low. With a potato masher, mash half can of each kind of bean until smooth. Add to saucepan. Add remaining beans. Simmer 20 to 30 minutes or until chicken is no longer pink and onion is tender. Top each serving with cheese.

When Kaden sleeps at Mom-Mom's house, this is one of his requests. It's flavorful and super healthy. If I'm really lucky she makes way too much and sends some home for me.

I've made sausage and kale soup many different ways, and this is my absolute favorite. It's not overly creamy, but that little touch of half-and-half makes all the difference. The kale cooks in the stock, so all the nutrients stay right in the soup. Ooh so good!

Sausage, Kale & White Bean Soup with Cream

Yield: 8 to 12 servings

1 pound uncooked mild Italian sausage, casings removed
1 small onion, chopped
6 garlic cloves, minced
4 to 6 celery stalks, chopped
6 cups chicken stock
1 (15-ounce) can white kidney beans (cannellini)
4 cups stemmed fresh kale
½ cup half-and-half

In a pot over medium-high heat, brown sausage, separating into crumbles with spatula or spoon. Drain grease and return sausage to heat. Add onion, garlic and celery; sauté until translucent, about 3 minutes. Add stock and bring to a boil. Reduce heat; cover and simmer 20 minutes. Add beans and kale; simmer an additional 5 minutes. Remove about ¼ cup soup and slowly mix with half-and-half (to temper). Slowly return soup and half-and-half mixture to pot; heat through (do not boil).

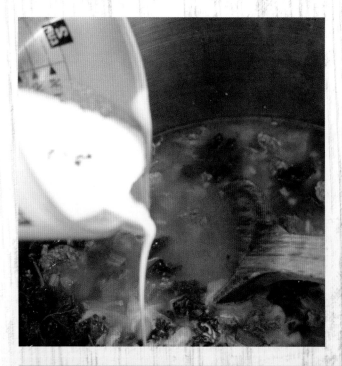

There's nothing like tomato soup and grilled cheese on a snow day. What happens when you forget to pick up a few cans of tomato soup for your cupboard and it's snowing? Well, you make your own. That's exactly what happened to me on our first middle-school snow day of the year. This recipe started out as me "winging it," but it is now one of our family favorites. Serve with a simple grilled cheese sandwich for a quick, comforting lunch or dinner any day of the week.

Quick & Simple Tomato Soup

Yield: 4 to 6 servings

2 tablespoons minced onion
1 tablespoon butter
1 (28-ounce) can crushed fire-roasted tomatoes
2 cups whole milk
1 cup vegetable broth

In a medium saucepan, cook onion in butter until tender. Add remaining ingredients. Simmer about 20 minutes. Remove from heat and purée in blender. Return to pan and gently simmer until heated through.

Cream of Broccoli Soup

4 stalks celery, chopped
1 large onion, chopped
3 tablespoons butter
2 heads fresh broccoli, trimmed and
coarsely chopped (about 8 cups)
2½ cups chicken broth
3 garlic cloves, chopped
1 teaspoon salt
White pepper to taste
2 tablespoons cornstarch
¼ cup cold water
2 cups half-and-half

In a large saucepan, sauté celery and onion in butter until tender. Add the broccoli, broth, garlic, salt and pepper; bring to a boil. Reduce heat; cover and simmer 25 to 30 minutes or until broccoli is tender. In a small bowl, combine cornstarch and water until smooth. Stir into soup. Bring to a boil; cook and stir 2 minutes or until thickened. Reduce heat to low. Stir in half-and-half; cook 10 minutes longer or until heated through. Remove half of the soup (about 3 cups) and purée in a food processor. Return to pot and stir.

My very first job in high school was at Kay's Italian Restaurant in Daleville, Pennsylvania. I started as a dishwasher and moved up to waitressing through college. One of my most special memories was the mornings I would come to work and Kay herself would be whipping up a batch of her famous Cream of Broccoli Soup for the soup of the day. Talk about a fabulous woman! She was Italian Fabulous as she ran around the restaurant in her high heels always looking glamorous. Kaden has grown to love this soup as well. I'm very lucky that my child is crazy about broccoli. It may be his favorite veggie. Who can say that? I've done my best here to replicate it but honestly, even if we're ordering a pizza, Kaden can't ever pass up a bowl of cream of broccoli soup from Kay's! Like mother, like son.

Stuffed Pepper Soup

Yield: 6 to 8 servings

1 pound lean ground beef
Salt and pepper to taste
½ medium onion, chopped
2 medium red bell peppers, chopped
1 large green bell pepper, chopped
4 garlic cloves, minced
4 cups beef stock
4 cups tomato sauce
1 (14.5-ounce) can crushed fire-roasted tomatoes
2 tablespoons raw sugar
1 cup cooked jasmine rice
1 tablespoon dried parsley
Grated Cheddar or mozzarella cheese
for serving, optional

Place beef in a large pot and season with salt and pepper. Cook, stirring occasionally while breaking up meat, until browned. Drain beef. Add onion, red bell pepper, green bell pepper and garlic and sauté until tender. Add beef stock and cook 15 to 20 minutes over medium heat. Add tomato sauce, crushed tomatoes and sugar. Cover and simmer on low heat, stirring occasionally, 30 minutes. Once soup is done, stir in cooked rice and parsley. Serve hot, topped with your choice of cheese.

If you enjoy stuffed peppers, then this soup is for you! It's very simple, has all the right flavors and, just like my stuffed peppers recipe, you can make this one in the slow cooker too (although I prefer it on the stove). If you choose the slow-cooker method, simply brown your beef first, drain, then toss everything in the slow cooker on low for 8 hours. It's comfort food at it's finest!

The story of a mother's life: Trapped between a scream and a hug. —Cathy Guisewite

Whether you grill it, fry it, bake it, broil it, or throw it in the crockpot, for most of us, a majority of our meals are centered around some kind of red meat. I've tried to live without it, but I just can't do it. Beef is one of my favorite things. Dad used to grill out on our deck in the middle of winter. I'm talking winter coat, winter boots, shovel a path in the snow, and crank up the grill. Back then, we only used charcoal, and the flavor was amazing. Imagine a dark snowy evening with the roar of the fire coming off the grill on the deck outside the kitchen window. It was quite an experience! Not to mention sitting down to a big, juicy New York strip steak in the middle of January. Yep, that was my dad. He enjoyed food and making things special even in the dead of winter when most people were throwing steaks in the broiler or cutting them up for a stew.

These days, it can feel like we're hamsters on a wheel. Running from one sporting event to another, helping with homework, bath, and bedtime. The thought of dinner becomes both overwhelming and exhausting. However, whether you realize it or not, your children will appreciate the meals you prepare for them. Maybe not right now but someday they'll look fondly upon the memories. Your efforts will be rewarded when they pass down recipes and traditions to their children. After all, I'm writing a whole book about my memories and recipes. I'm sure my mother never thought back then, as she was rushing to get food prepared for her family only to run out the door to work (and not even eating herself), that I would remember how special she made me feel, how I'd never forget those dinners.

A good steak or hamburger on the grill is definitely one of my favorite ways to ring in summer here on the East Coast. And there's nothing like a comforting slow-cooker meal on a cold winter day. I've transformed some of my all-time favorite beef recipes into slow-cooker superstars, as well as quick stove-top and oven-baked recipes to fit into any busy lifestyle. I hope you enjoy them as much as we do!

F2T Fabulous Tip: Make any night special by dressing up! Wear your Sunday best on a Wednesday. I spend a great deal of time in jammies or sweatpants because I spend a lot of time in my kitchen. Dressing up means we're going somewhere special so why not make a special night at home on a weeknight or weekend. Let the kids pick their own clothes and pretend you're dining in a castle. There's always something to celebrate so pick a reason if you really need one!

My son began eating ground beef only about a year ago. I have no idea why the aversion, but it didn't matter how I made it, he just wasn't having it. It wasn't until he went to his friend Karson's house for a birthday party that he came home loving hamburgers because "Karson's mom made the best!" Well, thank you, Karen, for getting Kaden to eat ground beef because not only can I make meatloaf again, but it may actually now be one of Kaden's favorite meals. Serve this delicious dish with my Twice-Baked Potatoes (page 190) for a complete meal or boil up some pasta; after all, it's Italian!

Italian Stuffed Meatloaf

Yield: 6 to 8 servings

2 pounds lean ground beef
1 egg
½ cup plain breadcrumbs
½ cup chopped onion
2 tablespoons ketchup
2 tablespoons Worcestershire sauce
2 tablespoons all-purpose seasoning
1 cup shredded mozzarella cheese
5 slices provolone cheese
1 cup tomato sauce, divided

Preheat oven to 400°. In a large bowl, combine first 7 ingredients; mix well. Divide into 2 equal parts. Place half into an ungreased 8x4-inch loaf pan, pressing meat up sides. Fill center with mozzarella, provolone and ½ cup tomato sauce. Place remaining meat mixture on top and seal edges to form a loaf. Top with remaining ½ cup tomato sauce. Bake 1 hour.

Steak Braciole

3 pounds beef top round, thinly sliced (or
flank steak pounded thin)
½ cup plain breadcrumbs
3 cups chopped fresh flat-leaf parsley
¼ cup grated Parmesan cheese
12 garlic cloves, minced
1 teaspoon dried oregano
Salt and pepper
4 tablespoons olive oil
4 to 6 cups spaghetti sauce
1 (6-ounce) can tomato paste
¼ cup red wine
Cooked pasta, optional

Flatten steak to ½-inch thickness by pounding with
a meat mallet, pounder or tenderizer. Combine
breadcrumbs, parsley, cheese, garlic, oregano and
¼ teaspoon each salt and pepper. Spoon over beef
to within 1 inch of edges; press down. Roll up jelly-
roll style, starting with long side; tie with kitchen
string or secure with toothpicks. In a pot, brown
meat in olive oil on all sides. Stir in spaghetti sauce,
tomato paste and wine. Bring to a boil. Reduce
heat to low; cover and simmer 70 to 80 minutes or
until meat is tender. (May also be transferred to a
slow cooker for 6 to 8 hours on low). Remove meat
from sauce and discard string (or toothpicks). Cut
into thin slices. Serve over prepared pasta topped
with sauce.

*This is a unique recipe many people may not have heard of, I realize, but it was a staple when I
was a kid. Once you try it, you will want it again and again. It's extra fun for kids because it's
a beef roll-up served in tomato sauce with pasta. The flavor is anything but a kid's meal as the
garlic permeates the meat and combines with fresh parsley to make it an incredibly flavorful
dish. It's melt-in-your-mouth tender and just plain scrumptious. My dad made this often, even
though it's Mom's recipe. I pair this dish with pasta since there's always plenty of sauce.*

This is one of the ultimate comfort foods, folks! Grab every different color pepper you can find in the farmers market, and it becomes quite a lovely meal as well. The peppers resemble a colorful bouquet of flowers, and since we first eat with our eyes, it's spectacular.

Stuffed Tricolored Peppers

Yield: 4 to 6 servings

6 large bell peppers (assorted green, red, orange and yellow)
3 cups tomato sauce, divided
1½ pounds ground beef
½ cup cooked rice
¼ cup chopped onion
1 egg
2 tablespoons all-purpose seasoning
Salt and pepper to taste

Gently remove tops and seeds from peppers. Set tops aside, removing stems. Rinse peppers. Turn over and carefully slice off uneven areas of the bottom, so they sit flat. (Be careful not to cut through peppers.) Pour 1 cup tomato sauce into slow cooker. In a bowl, combine beef, rice, onion, egg and seasonings. Divide 1 cup tomato sauce evenly between peppers, spooning sauce into bottom of each one. Stuff peppers with meat mixture; place in slow cooker. Top with remaining 1 cup tomato sauce and replace tops of peppers. Cook on low 8 hours.

Mom's Homemade Spaghetti Sauce and Meatballs

Yield: 4 to 6 servings

Meatballs:

2 to 3 pounds ground beef
¾ cup finely chopped onions
2 to 4 tablespoons parsley
½ cup breadcrumbs
1 teaspoon sweet basil
1 teaspoon oregano
1 to 2 eggs
Salt and pepper to taste
3 to 4 cloves very finely chopped
fresh garlic, optional

Spaghetti Sauce:

Olive oil
4 tablespoons chopped parsley
6 large cloves chopped fresh garlic
½ cup chopped onions
4 tablespoons chopped fresh celery leaves
1 teaspoon sweet basil
1 teaspoon oregano
Salt and pepper to taste
Dash rosemary
2 (6-ounce) cans tomato paste
2 (32-ounce) cans tomato purée
2 (32-ounce) cans tomato sauce
2 (32-ounce) cans crushed tomatoes

Mix all meatball ingredients together and form medium meatballs. Mixture should not be too dry or too moist so adjust ingredients as needed. To make spaghetti sauce, lightly cover bottom of a large pot with olive oil. Sauté all ingredients except tomato products over low heat until onions are translucent. Add meatballs and brown on all sides. You may have to do this in batches depending on how many meatballs you make. Add all meatballs back to the pot and add tomato products. Feel free to mix and match the tomato ingredients to make it your own family recipe. Simmer on low for 3 to 4 hours.

This recipe is so good that it was in the forward of my last cookbook and just for safe measure I'm including it in this one too. This is THE BEST spaghetti sauce and meatballs you will ever eat. It's my moms recipe so it's extra special to me. Whenever we would have company for dinner when I was little this was on the menu. My mom would start prepping in the morning and it would cook all day so the flavors blended beautifully. It really needs at least 3 to 4 hours to simmer so if you're planning to make this one, leave yourself some time. This isn't a weeknight meal unless you have some in your freezer. This is a get your ingredients a few days before, rainy day, cookin' in your jammie's kinda recipe. This is also the main ingredient in many other recipes throughout my book so if you're going to make it, make a lot of it and toss it in the freezer!

I mean, "set it and forget it," right? "Slow and low," yes? Who doesn't love a good slow-cooker meal? Better yet, who doesn't love a good pot roast on a cold or rainy day? That feeling of dinner being made when you get home takes the whole "what's for dinner" question off the table, pun intended. The secret to my slow-cooker recipes is to omit the onion. I know it's tempting to add onion, but to me, it makes all slow-cooker meals taste the same. Another trick is to reduce the sauce from the slow cooker on the stove. This recipe will be cooked in the gravy, so it will not be necessary to reduce it unless you would like it to be thicker.

Slow-Cooker Pot Roast with Smashed Potatoes

Yield: 6 servings

1 (2- to 3-pound) boneless chuck roast
½ teaspoon salt plus more to taste
¼ teaspoon pepper plus more to taste
2 tablespoons all-purpose seasoning
1 pound baby potatoes (I use tricolored)
4 tablespoons butter, divided
¼ cup red wine
1 teaspoon Worcestershire sauce
3 cups beef stock
4 tablespoons cornstarch
4 garlic cloves
¼ cup milk

Rub roast with salt, pepper and seasoning. Brown on all sides in pan over medium-high heat. Remove and place in slow cooker with potatoes on top. Return pan to heat; add 2 tablespoons butter to melt. Add wine, Worcestershire and stock to deglaze. In a separate bowl, whisk cornstarch in ½ cup water. Whisk into stock mixture. Pour sauce over roast and potatoes; add garlic. Cook on low 7 to 8 hours. Remove cooked potatoes. In a bowl, combine potatoes, remaining 2 tablespoons butter and milk. Roughly mash. Spread on a serving platter and season to taste with salt and pepper. Top with pot roast and gravy.

I stumbled upon this recipe years ago and have tweaked it numerous times since then. This recipe is for a night when you feel like a good steak but don't feel like cooking on the grill. The pan drippings make a perfect base for your sauce and the balsamic takes it to a whole new level. It's easy enough to make any night of the week, and the mushrooms are an extra side dish. Add a tossed salad and a baked sweet potato for a complete meal.

Balsamic-Glazed Filet Mignon

Yield: 6 servings

3 tablespoons olive oil
3 (4- to 6-ounce) beef tenderloin steaks
¾ teaspoon salt
½ teaspoon pepper
4 tablespoons butter
1 shallot, thinly sliced
3 cups beef stock
3 to 4 cups sliced shiitake, baby bella and crimini mushrooms
2 tablespoons balsamic vinegar

Drizzle olive oil in a large skillet or grill pan over medium heat. Season steaks with salt and pepper; place in pan. Cook 6 to 8 minutes on each side to desired doneness. (For medium rare, a thermometer should read 145°; medium, 160°; well done, 170°. Keep in mind that the meat may cook additionally while resting.) Remove to a plate, cover and set aside. To the pan, add butter and shallot. Cook until clear, scraping bits from pan. Gradually whisk in stock. Bring to a boil. Cook until sauce reduces and thickens, approximately 20 minutes. Add mushrooms and balsamic vinegar. Cook 3 to 5 minutes. Place steaks back in the pan. Cover with sauce and mushrooms. Serve right from the pan or on a platter.

Golabki (Beef-Stuffed Cabbage Rolls)

Yield: 4 to 6 servings

1 medium head cabbage
2 pounds ground beef
1 cup cooked rice
1 small onion, finely chopped
2 eggs
2 teaspoons salt
½ teaspoon pepper
1 (28-ounce) can crushed fire-roasted tomatoes

Place whole cabbage in a large pot of water. Bring to a boil and cook until tender throughout, 25 to 35 minutes. In a bowl, combine ground beef, rice, onion, eggs and seasonings; mix well. Remove cabbage from pot and let cool slightly. Remove core and slowly pull apart from the center out to loosen leaves. Remove leaves carefully and set aside. Put about ¼ to ½ cup meat mixture on each cabbage leaf. Fold in sides; starting at an unfolded edge, roll up leaf to completely enclose filling. Repeat with remaining leaves and filling. Place rolls in a slow cooker with half the crushed tomatoes on the bottom. Pour remaining crushed tomatoes over cabbage rolls along with 1 cup water. Cook 6 to 7 hours on low.

When Mom would say, "Grandma Kenosky called, and we're going down to her house for dinner tonight," I would get so excited. My grandmother was 100 percent Italian and my grandfather was 100 percent Polish, so you could tell she perfected her version of Golabki for her Polish hubby. This recipe takes a little time but don't despair. It's really not as difficult as everyone makes it sound. Once you get into a rhythm it will be easy-peasy, and the good news is that you'll definitely have leftovers, so all your effort will be so worth it when you're eating them the next day. This is the perfect Sunday supper or make it on Sunday to slow cook Monday. This recipe contains your meat, starch, and veggie, so all you need is some fresh bread and butter for a scrumptious meal.

I would give anything to once again have one of Grandma Kenosky's hamburgers with fried onion to enjoy with an RC cola, in a can, and a Nestlé chocolate bar. My grandparents owned a small bar, and my grandmother would cook on occasion for her patrons. When we stopped by, she would always make us one of her special burgers. It was also a reward for a job well done after we cut her grass in the summertime. She had the biggest yard ever, so it was well deserved. The secret to her burgers? Well, Grandma always said to use a wet slice of bread rather than breadcrumbs, and, boy, was she right. Add your favorite chips and a pickle to complete this quick yet satisfying meal.

Grandma Kenosky's Hamburger with Fried Onion

Yield: 4 to 6 servings

1 pound ground beef
1 slice white bread, soaked in water
1 large egg, beaten
½ to 1 teaspoon salt
⅛ teaspoon pepper
2 tablespoons olive oil
1 small onion, sliced

In a large bowl, combine ground beef, bread, egg, salt and pepper; mix well. Shape into 4 to 6 patties. Drizzle oil in a skillet; add onions. Add burgers and cook to desired doneness. Remove hamburgers and pat with paper towel to remove any excess oil. Place on a bun and top with onion. Serve immediately.

Optional: Cook these in mini patties then melt cheese on top. Serve on slider buns topped with pickles. Mini Cheeseburger Sliders will be a hit with the kids and the adults.

Herb-Crusted New York Strip Steak Salad

Yield: 4 to 6 servings

Steak:

3 tablespoons olive oil
3 tablespoons all-purpose seasoning
1 teaspoon mustard powder
Salt and pepper to taste
2 (1-pound) boneless
New York strip steaks

Dressing:

1 tablespoon Dijon mustard
1 teaspoon honey
3 tablespoons balsamic vinegar
½ cup olive oil
4 ounces blue cheese crumbles
Salt and pepper to taste

Salad:

2 heads Boston or Bibb lettuce
½ red onion, sliced
2 tomatoes, chopped

Drizzle oil in grill pan over medium heat. Combine steak seasonings and rub on both sides of steaks. Place in pan and cook 6 to 8 minutes each side or until desired doneness. In a bowl, whisk ingredients together for salad dressing. Combine salad ingredients on a platter and toss with dressing. Serve steaks in pan with salad on the side or slice steak to place on top of salad.

Kaden loves to help cook, and one of his specialties is herb-crusted anything! It's how he almost landed a spot on the "Kid's BBQ Challenge" on the Food Network. Well, the recipe and his sparkling personality of course! It was winter at the time, so cooking on the grill was a bit of a challenge for my little man and moving it inside to a grill pan was equally challenging. It's a tricky technique for a little guy, but we were very proud of his efforts. He did an amazing job and almost made it on the show with his delicious, juicy, herb-crusted chicken. These days, he continues to practice his culinary skills in the kitchen, and he's certainly right. Those herbs sure give any meat remarkable flavor, especially this New York strip steak.

Meatloaf is the quintessential comfort food. This meatloaf is not only delicious, but it's so super simple that you can whip it up when you get home from a busy day. My mom's meatloaf was always a crowd-pleaser in my family and still is to this day.

Classic Meatloaf

Yield: 4 servings

1½ pounds ground beef
1 egg
½ cup plain breadcrumbs
4 tablespoons ketchup, divided
1 tablespoon Worcestershire sauce
1 tablespoon Dijon mustard
½ cup chopped onion
1 small red bell pepper, chopped
½ teaspoon garlic powder
Salt and pepper to taste

Preheat oven to 400°. Combine all ingredients, using 2 tablespoons ketchup, in a bowl. Press into a loaf and place in an ungreased loaf pan. Spread remaining 2 tablespoons ketchup on top. Bake 45 minutes or until no longer pink inside.

My Mother taught me to walk proud and tall as if the world was mine. —Sophia Loren

There are many ways to prepare chicken, and because it's my favorite thing to eat (next to seafood), I've included a few extra recipes. It's a very cost-effective option, especially when you purchase chicken in bulk and repackage it for the freezer. Another bonus to chicken is that it cooks so quickly, so it's perfect for the busy mom. Growing up on a chicken farm inspired the passion for my farm-to-table style of cooking. Of course, because my grandparents were farmers, they were very practical and utilized everything (and I do mean everything). However, I can honestly say I have no recollection of how the chicken actually made it to the table, which is probably a good thing according to my cousins. I think it's because I'm able to block out that memory that I enjoy chicken so much today. If you ask my aunts and uncles, they may have a different opinion. Most of the chickens were used for their eggs only, sold out of my grandparents' roadside stand, so I like to focus on that wonderful aspect of the farm. Farmer Storm's Stand, as it was called, was one of my favorite places on the planet. It was where you could always find my grandma, her warm smile and a hug, as well as my grandpa in from the fields for lunch every day at noon.

One of my favorite memories of the farm was when Grandpa let us help feed the baby chicks or "peeps" as we called them. They were so sweet and tiny. In my childhood memories, I swear there were thousands of them around our feet. Grandpa let us help feed the chickens quite often and it was wonderful to have one-on-one time with him. He was a kind, sweet, gentle man with the bluest eyes I'd ever seen. You could always find a smile on his face and in those eyes. Another of my favorite memories is when we helped move chickens from one coop to another. Grandpa would fire up the tractor complete with hay wagon, and we would all grab a chicken to transport across the farm. It was a family affair, so it didn't take too many trips. We have a very big family. It was an honest-to-goodness hayride complete with chickens that really didn't want to be in anyone's arms. It was always an occasion with many laughs for that very reason. Grandma always followed up with a warm meal at the farmhouse as a thank you for our help.

Nowadays, I don't have to work quite as hard for my meal as we're lucky enough to carry delicious organic chicken in our markets. It's a go-to meal for me on many occasions because it's so readily available (and already packaged). I'm lucky enough to get to prepare it in the same kitchen as my grandma did all those years ago.

F2T Fabulous Tip: Have a theme night complete with costumes. Use superhero jammies, left-over Halloween costumes or something from one of your kiddo's birthday parties. Yep, you guessed it Mom and Dad, you're dressing up too. There are many themes you can choose, and it's a fun way to make dinner a little extra special. And if you happen to have some Star Wars-themed paper plates, why not use them? Pick your theme and celebrate, and don't forget the music.

Chicken Fajitas with Fresh Veggies

Yield: 6 servings

2 tablespoons white wine vinegar
2 tablespoons fresh lime juice
1 tablespoon vegetable oil
plus more for vegetables
1 garlic clove, minced
¼ teaspoon ground cumin
½ teaspoon salt, optional
1 pound boneless, skinless chicken strips
1 medium green pepper, sliced
1 medium sweet red pepper, sliced
1 medium sweet onion, sliced
6 (8-inch) flour tortillas
½ cup sour cream
Guacamole, salsa and shredded Cheddar
cheese, optional

In a large resealable plastic bag or glass container, combine vinegar, lime juice, 1 tablespoon oil, garlic, cumin and salt, if desired. Add chicken. Cover or close bag and refrigerate at least 4 hours. Drain, discarding marinade. Lightly oil vegetables. Grill vegetables and chicken, uncovered, over medium heat 12 to 15 minutes or until vegetables begin to soften and chicken juices run clear. Meanwhile, warm tortillas according to package directions. Spread each tortilla lightly with sour cream. Spoon chicken and vegetables down the center and fold in sides. Garnish as desired with guacamole, salsa and cheese.

This is a fun and easy dinner. The kiddos can help prep the veggies while you cook the chicken. Chicken Fajitas are easy to take outdoors for a fun family night dinner so you don't have to worry about how messy they can be. As a matter of fact, break out the paper plates for this dinner. You have my permission.

I love balsamic vinegar on just about anything when I'm looking for extra flavor. This is a very easy recipe that doesn't look like or taste like it was easy to prepare. There's no need to prep before because, yes, it's that simple. Pour a nice glass of wine with this one, mommies, because you're going to feel like you're at a restaurant. I think it's the perfect night to have your family clean up too. Serve with a side of Roasted Veggies (170), which are equally delicious with a little balsamic drizzle.

Balsamic-Glazed Chicken Breast

Yield: 4 to 6 servings

1 tablespoon olive oil
4 (4- to 5-ounce) boneless, skinless
chicken breasts, halved
Salt and pepper
4 tablespoons butter
1 shallot, finely chopped
3 cups chicken stock
1 to 2 cups assorted mushrooms, optional
2 tablespoons balsamic vinegar

In a pan, heat oil over medium heat. Season chicken to taste with salt and pepper; add to pan. Cook 20 to 25 minutes, turning once, until juices run clear and internal temperature reaches 165°. Remove from pan and cover. In the same pan, add butter and scrape chicken bits from bottom of the pan. Add shallot. Cook until transparent and fragrant. Add chicken stock, turn heat to high and cook until liquid is reduced by at least half. Sauce will thicken. Add mushrooms to pan, tossing until heated and tender, about 5 minutes. Add balsamic vinegar and cook about 2 to 3 minutes, being careful not to burn the vinegar. Pour balsamic glaze over chicken breasts and serve.

Roasted Chicken Thighs & Legs

Yield: 8 servings

8 boneless, skinless chicken thighs
(about 2 pounds)
6 chicken drumsticks (about 1 pound)
6 to 8 garlic cloves, roughly chopped
4 sprigs fresh rosemary
3 tablespoons olive oil
2 teaspoons all-purpose seasoning
½ teaspoon salt
¼ teaspoon pepper

Preheat oven to 375°. Place chicken in casserole dish or pan with garlic and rosemary. Toss with oil to coat. Sprinkle with all-purpose seasoning, salt and pepper. Roast, uncovered, 45 to 60 minutes, turning once, until a thermometer inserted in chicken reads 170° and chicken is golden brown.

On nights my grandma Kenosky called on a whim to invite us to dinner, this was one of my absolute favorites. The roasted garlic makes the house smell so good. To me, rosemary smells like a Christmas tree so it's nostalgic for many reasons. Not to mention, the prep takes, maybe, 15 minutes. I mean, wow! It's also a one-pot dish so just add a salad, like Grandma used to, and you have a well-rounded meal.

We love our chicken wings here in northeastern Pennsylvania! However, they're not terribly healthy, so it's not something we eat too often....until now. Thanks to the air fryer, we've removed the deep-frying step entirely to make it a bit healthier. Now I didn't say this was necessarily low-cal. After all, every good chicken wing needs a savory sauce. I promise that this sauce will not disappoint. Every time I make this recipe for my boys, they tell me it's the best version of a chicken wing they've ever tasted. What busy mom doesn't like to hear that every once in a while? Serve alone or with crispy kale for a complete meal.

Crispy Garlic-Parmesan Chicken Wings

Yield: 2 servings

Dry Rub:

1 teaspoon garlic powder
1 teaspoon onion powder
1 teaspoon paprika
½ teaspoon salt
½ teaspoon sage
½ teaspoon thyme

Chicken Wings:

12 whole chicken wings
3 garlic cloves, finely chopped
4 tablespoons butter
1 cup white wine (something you like to drink, preferably dry or semisweet)
½ cup grated Parmesan cheese

Combine Rub ingredients in a small bowl. Toss wings in rub. Place in air fryer at 380° for 40 to 45 minutes, turning once, until crispy (or until internal temperature reaches 165° and is no longer pink). In a separate pan, sauté garlic in butter over low heat until fragrant, 3 to 5 minutes. Add wine and turn heat to high until sauce thickens, about 10 minutes. In a bowl, toss chicken wings in sauce and Parmesan cheese. Serve hot.

This is one of my mother's specialties. I'm not going to lie, this is one of those "extra effort" recipes that is totally worth the extra work. You will have leftovers, so you'll get the next night off. A night off from cooking for a busy mom is a gift, in my opinion. These chicken strips freeze very well in a zip-close bag and can be made the day before, so all you have to do is heat them up. Serve over rice or mashed potatoes for a delicious dinner any night of the week.

Chicken Strips in Wine, Butter & Garlic

Yield: 6 servings

2 cups all-purpose flour
Salt and pepper to taste
1½ to 2 pounds boneless, skinless chicken tenders
1 cup olive oil
2 tablespoons butter
½ cup chopped onion
6 garlic cloves, minced
3 cups chicken broth
½ cup white wine
2 cups cooked jasmine rice
2 tablespoons chopped fresh parsley

Add flour to a zip-close bag; season with salt and pepper. Working in batches, add chicken tenders and toss to coat. Preheat oil in pan over medium heat. Shake excess flour off tenders and place in pan. Cook until golden brown, turning once, about 10 to 15 minutes. Remove from pan and place on paper towel. In a clean pan, cook butter, onion and garlic until onion is translucent; do not brown. Add chicken broth, wine and tenders to pan. Cook 15 to 20 minutes until sauce thickens. Serve over rice and top with parsley.

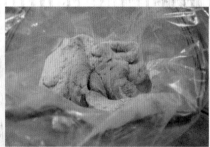

Homemade Chicken Pot Pie

2 stalks celery, chopped
1 large potato, peeled and cubed
2 tablespoons butter
1 boneless, skinless chicken breast
1 bay leaf
1 (16-ounce) bag frozen mixed vegetables
1 (14.5-ounce) can chicken stock
2 tablespoons flour
2 (9-inch) refrigerated pie crusts

Combine all ingredients, except flour and pie crusts, in a slow cooker and cook on high 3 hours (6 hours on low). Place one crust in a 9-inch pie plate. Add flour to filling in slow cooker and mix well, shredding chicken. Spoon filling into crust. Top with remaining pie crust and seal edges by pinching with finger tips. Bake at 425° for 45 minutes or until lightly browned. Let stand 5 minutes before serving.

At this moment, Kaden is obsessed with video games and chicken pot pie. I'm not so fond of the video games, but I do love a nice healthy, hearty pot pie. It's the nutritional equivalent of chicken soup and takes me back to wonderful childhood memories. As a child, if it was chicken pot pie night, we were most certainly eating on TV trays in the living room. It was something we didn't do often, so it was a treat. Nowadays, as much as we try to sit down as a family, every now and again we do end up in the living room. Maybe I should pick up some TV trays? Hmmmm, food for thought! Pun intended.

This is a great dinner for all children and is tasty enough for adults, too. For Kaden, I generally double the recipe. Toss these in the air fryer for a quick go-to meal any night of the week. Add a piece of fruit and some sweet potato fries for a complete dinner for even the pickiest eater.

Breaded Chicken Tenders

Yield: 4 servings

1 pound boneless, skinless chicken breasts
4 tablespoons melted butter
1 cup seasoned breadcrumbs

Slice chicken into tenders. Place butter in a resealable plastic bag. Place breadcrumbs in a second bag. Shake chicken pieces in butter, then breadcrumbs to coat. Place in air fryer at 370° for 15 to 20 minutes. Serve with your kid's favorite dipping sauce.

Chicken Nugget & Fruit Kabobs

Yield: 4 servings

1 cup seasoned breadcrumbs
4 tablespoons melted butter
1 pound boneless, skinless chicken
breasts, cut into 1-inch cubes
16 strawberries
1 green apple, cut into chunks and
tossed in lemon juice
16 cherry tomatoes
16 to 24 cubes your favorite cheese

In a large resealable plastic bag, place breadcrumbs. In a separate bag, place melted butter. Add chicken to bag with butter. Shake chicken pieces in butter, then breadcrumbs to coat. Place in air fryer at 370° for 15 to 20 minutes. Thread 4 skewers with chicken, fruit, tomatoes and cheese until each skewer has equal amounts of each ingredient.

This simple dish served at most fast-food restaurants is taken to a whole new level simply by adding fruit, veggies or both. You can serve the kabobs with your favorite dipping sauces from barbecue to honey mustard and ranch to marinara. Kids love color, and we all know that we eat with our eyes first. When they feast their eyes on these beautiful masterpieces, they'll be asking for more! What's more, it's a complete meal so no need for sides.

Chicken Cordon Bleu

2 (4- to 6-pound) boneless, skinless
chicken breasts
4 slices deli ham
4 slices Gruyère or Swiss cheese
½ cup dry breadcrumbs
½ teaspoon salt
⅛ teaspoon paprika

Slice each chicken breast in half lengthwise; flatten each of the 4 pieces to ¼-inch thickness. Top each with ham and cheese. Roll up and tuck in ends; secure with toothpicks. In a shallow bowl, combine breadcrumbs, salt and paprika. Roll chicken in crumb mixture. Transfer to a greased 8-inch-square baking dish. Bake at 350° for 40 to 45 minutes (turning once) or until chicken juices run clear. Discard toothpicks.

This dish may sound fancy, but it's easier to make than you think and can be whipped up in minutes. To children, they're simply a meat roll-up, so they will love this for dinner. These days you can buy your chicken already thinly sliced and if for some reason you can't find it, ask your butcher to slice it thinly for you. I mean, who really wants to pound chicken unless it's absolutely necessary? Serve with my Sautéed Spinach & Garlic (page 175) or Cabbage & Noodles (page 189) for the perfect meal.

When we order takeout (yes, even the farm-to-table fabulous gal orders takeout), Chicken Parmigiana is one of our faves. We're working moms. No one wants to cook every night. Chicken Parmigiana is good homemade, too. I serve it with a side of angel hair pasta or on a bed of roasted kale.

Chicken Parmigiana

Yield: 4 servings

2 (4-ounce) boneless, skinless chicken breasts
1½ cups plain dry breadcrumbs
½ cup grated Parmesan cheese
4 slices provolone cheese
1 (28-ounce) can crushed tomatoes
1½ teaspoons garlic powder
1 cup shredded mozzarella cheese

Slice each chicken breast in half lengthwise. Place breadcrumbs and Parmesan in a bowl. Dredge chicken in breadcrumb mixture to evenly coat. Place in an ungreased 9x13-inch baking dish. Bake, uncovered, at 400° for 25 to 30 minutes or until chicken juices run clear. Top each chicken breast with provolone. In a saucepan, heat crushed tomatoes; stir in garlic powder. Cover chicken with warm crushed tomatoes and sprinkle with mozzarella. Bake 5 to 10 minutes longer or until cheese is melted.

Chicken Caprese

2 tablespoons olive oil, divided
2 (4- to 6-ounce) boneless, skinless chicken breasts, halved
4 garlic cloves, chopped
1 cup balsamic vinegar or balsamic glaze
2 cups cherry or grape tomatoes
1 cup shredded mozzarella cheese
Torn fresh basil or parsley leaves

In a pan, heat 1 tablespoon oil over medium-high heat. Brown chicken on both sides. Cook until thermometer reads 165°. Remove from heat; set chicken aside. In same pan, cook garlic in remaining 1 tablespoon oil until fragrant, 3 to 5 minutes. Add balsamic vinegar and tomatoes. Cook until tomatoes begin to wilt. Return chicken to pan. Spoon vinegar and tomatoes over chicken. Top with cheese and cover pan with lid until cheese is melted. Top with basil or parsley and serve immediately.

Easy peasy, fresh and cheesy. This is seriously one of the simplest yet gratifying dishes to make. It's packed full of flavor and beautiful. I personally like it in the summertime with fresh cherry or grape tomatoes and fresh basil or parsley. It's also nice if you want to get a babysitter and have a girls' night-in with everyone bringing a dish. Serve with a bottle of crisp white wine and don't forget the chocolate for dessert.

I just love cooking with lemon. It's such a fresh, vibrant flavor. If you can't find chicken sliced thin (or scaloppini-style), then you will have to pound the chicken. This recipe cooks very quickly, and if you serve it with rice, you have a beautiful dinner in no time.

Chicken Francese

Yield: 4 servings

2 boneless, skinless chicken breasts, halved
3 large eggs
1 cup flour
3 tablespoons butter, divided
2 lemons, divided
2 cups chicken stock
Salt and pepper to taste

Pound chicken breasts with a meat mallet to ¼-inch thickness; slice into cutlets 1½ inches wide. Beat eggs in a shallow bowl; place flour in a separate shallow bowl. In a large skillet, heat 2 tablespoons butter over medium heat. Working in batches, dip chicken in egg; coat with flour. Brown in skillet until golden brown, about 2 to 3 minutes per side. Remove from pan and set aside. Add juice and zest from 1 lemon to skillet along with chicken stock; stir to loosen browned bits from pan. Bring to a boil over medium-high heat. Reduce heat; simmer, uncovered, until liquid is reduced by half, 8 to 10 minutes. Return chicken to pan; toss to coat. Season with salt and pepper. Cook until heated through, 4 to 6 minutes. Turn off heat and stir in remaining butter until melted. Slice remaining lemon and use as garnish.

Chicken Stir-Fry

Yield: 4 servings

1 pound boneless, skinless chicken breasts, cut into strips
1 tablespoon sesame oil
2 garlic cloves, minced
1 medium zucchini, sliced
1 medium red bell pepper, sliced
3 tablespoons soy sauce, divided
2 tablespoons chopped scallion for garnish

In a large skillet or wok, stir-fry chicken in oil 10 to 15 minutes or until juices run clear. Add garlic, zucchini, pepper and 2 tablespoons soy sauce. Cover and simmer 7 to 9 minutes or until vegetables are tender. Top with scallions and remaining soy sauce.

This is a fun meal for the kids, especially if you find those cute little baby corns. It seems kids love anything little. This Chicken Stir-Fry is also ready in minutes. Don't have a wok? No problem. I've used a skillet many times, and it's still incredibly delicious. Add rice noodles or jasmine rice for a complete meal. Grab some chopsticks and dig in!

My grandma Storm never wasted anything, especially food. If we had a chicken for dinner, we would most likely get together the next night for chicken and dumplings. You can double, even triple, this recipe so invite family over to make memories of your own. This is a "make on Sunday while you're cleaning the house" kind of busy mom's Sunday dinner.

Chicken & Dumplings

Yield: 4 to 6 servings

Chicken:

4 boneless chicken breast cutlets
4 to 6 boneless, skinless chicken thighs
1 tablespoon all-purpose seasoning
1 cup chicken broth
2 (14-ounce) cans cream of mushroom soup
3 celery stalks, chopped
3 medium carrots, sliced
1 (10-ounce) bag frozen peas
1 bay leaf
Salt and pepper to taste

Dumplings:

1 cup all-purpose flour
2 teaspoons baking powder
1 teaspoon sugar
½ teaspoon salt
1 tablespoon margarine
½ cup milk

Combine chicken, all-purpose seasoning, chicken broth and soup in a slow cooker. Cook on high 3 hours. Remove lid. Pull apart meat into large pieces, not entirely shredded. Add celery, carrots, peas, bay leaf, salt and pepper.

Prepare Dumplings by stirring together flour, baking powder, sugar and salt in a medium-size bowl. Cut in margarine until crumbly. Stir in milk to make a soft dough. Drop by teaspoonfuls into slow cooker. Cover and cook an additional hour on high.

This is a quick, delicious, and healthy way to make sure your kiddos eat their greens. Ever since our Farm to Table Valentine's Dinner at the market a couple years ago, I'm slightly obsessed with stuffing chicken with just about anything. It's a great way to layer flavors without having to fuss over side dishes. Add a starch, such as a smashed red potato or simple baked potato, for a complete and satisfying meal.

Parmesan-Crusted Chicken Breast

Yield: 4 servings

4 boneless, skinless chicken breasts, pocketed for stuffing
⅛ teaspoon each salt and pepper
2 cups arugula
1 cup halved grape tomatoes
½ cup shredded mozzarella cheese
¾ cup plus 2 tablespoons grated Parmesan, divided
4 tablespoons balsamic vinegar
2 tablespoons Dijon mustard

Preheat oven to 450°. Season chicken with salt and pepper; set aside. In a bowl, combine arugula, tomatoes, mozzarella and 2 tablespoons Parmesan. Toss together. Stuff a quarter of arugula mixture into each chicken breast. Place remaining ¾ cup Parmesan in a shallow bowl; add salt and pepper to taste. Evenly coat each stuffed chicken breast with seasoned cheese and place in a shallow baking dish. Bake approximately 40 minutes (or until internal temperature reaches 170°), turning once. In a separate bowl, whisk together vinegar and mustard. Pour over chicken and cook an additional 5 minutes. Spoon sauce from pan over chicken and serve.

Grilled Marinated Italian Chicken

Yield: 4 to 6 servings

1 (16-ounce) bottle Ken's Italian dressing
6 garlic cloves, roughly chopped
4 (4- to 6-ounce) boneless skinless chicken breasts, halved

In a large resealable plastic bag, combine dressing and garlic. Add chicken; seal bag and turn to coat. Refrigerate 8 hours or overnight. Drain and discard marinade. Place chicken in a grill pan or on a grill and cook over medium heat 6 to 8 minutes on each side or until a meat thermometer reads 170°.

I love a good vinegar-based marinade for chicken on the grill. We have such a short summer here in northeastern Pennsylvania that we love to take advantage of the grilling season by eating outside whenever the weather allows. Starting the marinade process the day before making it super easy to just pull the chicken out of the fridge and throw it on the grill with some fresh veggies and you have dinner in minutes. A perfect meal for eating by the pool or lake while your kids take a dip between bites. That's my kind of summer night!

This recipe is super simple yet full of flavor. For those of you organized enough to prep meals ahead of time over the weekend, you could always brown the chicken in large batches then make the sauce fresh before serving. Serve with Roasted Veggies (page 170) or rice for a complete meal.

Chicken Dijon

Yield: 2 to 4 servings

½ cup half-and-half
¼ cup Dijon mustard
1 tablespoon honey
2 (4- to 6-ounce) boneless,
skinless chicken breasts, halved
¼ teaspoon salt
¼ teaspoon pepper
2 teaspoons olive oil
2 teaspoons butter
Minced fresh scallions

Whisk together half-and-half, mustard and honey. Pound chicken breasts with a meat mallet to even thickness; sprinkle with salt and pepper. In a large pan, heat oil and butter over medium-high heat; brown chicken on both sides. Reduce heat to medium. Add half-and-half mixture; bring to a boil. Reduce heat; simmer, covered, until internal chicken temperature reaches 165°, approximately 10 to 12 minutes. Sprinkle with scallions.

Chicken Piccata

1 cup flour
2 (4- to 6-ounce) boneless, skinless
chicken breasts, butterflied
2 tablespoons olive oil
½ cup chicken stock
⅓ cup white wine
1 lemon, juiced
½ cup capers (with brine)
2 tablespoons butter
Salt to taste

Place flour in a zip-close bag. Place chicken in bag, seal and shake until evenly coated. Shake off excess flour and place in skillet with olive oil over medium heat. Cook 4 to 5 minutes on each side until juices run clear. Remove chicken from pan and set aside. In same pan, add chicken stock, white wine and lemon juice. Scape up any bits from pan. Place chicken back in pan and cook until sauce is thickened, about 10 minutes. Turn off heat, stir in capers , butter and salt until heated thoroughly.

This Chicken Piccata sounds a little fancy but is really easy—my kind of recipe. Who doesn't like to look like a superstar without working in the kitchen for hours? I love this dish served with my Crispy Herb-Roasted Potatoes (page 195) and Roasted Veggies (page 170). Just throw everything in the oven while you work on the sauce, and before you know it, dinner is served, superstar!

And all thy children shall be taught of the Lord; and great shall be the peace of thy children. —Isaiah 54:13

Who doesn't remember that line "pork chops and applesauce," uttered by the one and only Peter Brady of the popular sitcom The Brady Bunch? I'm sure my child (and most of this generation) won't get it, but if you grew up in the '70s, you were probably watching reruns, like me, of this famous TV family. That episode was one of my favorites. Now let's get back to pork, the other white meat. It's so versatile. Whether you stuff it, barbecue it, grill it, give it some Asian flare, or just bake it, it's really a nice option for dinner anytime of the year. Living in northeastern Pennsylvania, we rely on comfort food to see us through the long winter months.

One of the busiest moms I knew was Grandma Storm, grandmom of ten who were always at her house. I don't think I remember a moment when she wasn't wearing her apron. Grandma loved to use her cast-iron skillet on top of her wood stove. I remember the smell of wood burning, along with a delicious meal cooking, like it was yesterday. She had a stove in her home as well as the farm stand. She always made homemade meals even during a busy work day. My grandpa would come in from the fields for lunch every single day. They always sat down at the table for something hot and homemade. In my opinion, nothing sears better than a nice, thick pork chop in a cast-iron skillet, and no one made it better than Grandma Storm.

I love a good, old-fashioned, breaded pork chop. It's my personal favorite way to eat pork—basic, nostalgic, and delicious. One of my son's favorite ways to eat pork is barbecue style. Kaden absolutely loves barbecue ribs and pulled pork barbecue. The excitement on his face when I tell him we're having pork barbecue for dinner is unlike any other. It's pure, authentic joy. I love to make a memory, and the way to do that in my family is through their bellies. I know my son will always remember his mom's pork barbecue.

F2T Fabulous Tip: Take the kids on a little treasure hunt outside (or the grocery store or local farmers market) for something for your table's centerpiece. I like to use apples or pears from my fruit trees; purchased fruit works great too. Hand-picked flowers look great in a vase. In winter, the treasure may simply be holly branches. There's nothing like a little added beauty to your table to make an ordinary night extraordinary.

Oh, happy day it was when I would come home from school and see this on the stove under tin foil. This candied ham served with Mom's scalloped potatoes was one of my favorite meals. Using a precooked and presliced ham means you can make this delicious dinner even on a weeknight. You're really just heating it up and allowing the brown sugar mixture to thicken and permeate the meat.

Candied Ham with Glazed Carrots

Yield: 6 to servings

1 (2-pound) fully cooked, presliced ham
(or 1 quarter ham)
2 cups baby carrots
1 cup packed brown sugar, divided
Juice from 1 orange
4 tablespoons butter

Preheat oven to 400°. Place ham slices, overlapping, in a shallow 9x13-inch casserole dish. Place carrots on top. In a small pot, combine ½ cup brown sugar, orange juice and butter on low heat until bubbly. Pour over ham and carrots. Cover with foil and bake 30 to 40 minutes until carrots are tender. (To save time, you may skip the next step if you prefer a thinner sauce and lighter ham.) Remove foil; top with remaining ½ cup brown sugar. Bake, uncovered, an additional 30 minutes until sauce thickens and ham browns.

Pork Dumplings

Yield: 52 dumplings

1 pound fully cooked boneless
pork loin chops, diced
1 green onion, chopped
½ white cabbage, roughly chopped
2 tablespoons rice vinegar
1 teaspoon ground ginger
1 tablespoon sesame oil
1 tablespoon soy sauce
1 (12-ounce) package wonton wrappers

Place the first 7 ingredients in a food processor; process until finely chopped. Place 2 teaspoons pork mixture in the center of a wonton wrapper. (Keep remaining wrappers covered with a damp paper towel until ready to use.) Moisten edges with water. Bring corners of wonton wrapper over filling and twist to form a bundle; pinch edges to seal. Repeat. Fill a large saucepan three-quarters full of water. Cover and bring to a boil. Place about 6 dumplings in water and cook 10 to 12 minutes or until they float. Remove to a serving bowl. Repeat until all dumplings are cooked. Combine Dipping Sauce ingredients; serve with hot dumplings.

Dipping Sauce:
¼ cup soy sauce
1 tablespoon honey
1½ teaspoons finely chopped green onion
½ teaspoon sesame oil

I was always intimidated by the thought of making Asian dumplings. To me, they were something to eat as an appetizer when going out to dinner. In that way, they're special. We have a local Asian restaurant that is Kaden's favorite and is typically where we go for his reward dinner for a good report card. I realized how easy it is to make dumplings at home while testing recipes for my first cookbook. You can make these the night before or even over the weekend to freeze for a weeknight dinner. Just place them on wax paper on a baking sheet and freeze. They're very filling, and with a little salad, make a great, well-rounded meal.

This is a lovely seasonal meal for fall. In addition to apple stuffing, I love a good fall baseball game on a cool, crisp autumn night with my hands wrapped around a hot chocolate. We don't mind firing up the oven here in the fall since it's usually freezing by September. This can be prepped the night before so all you have to do is throw it in the oven when you get home after a busy day or a nail-biting game.

Stuffed Pork Chops

Yield: 6 servings

¼ cup butter
3 cups soft bread cubes
2 tart apples, chopped
¼ cup finely chopped celery
2 tablespoons chopped pecans
Salt and pepper to taste
6 (1½-inch-thick) pork loin chops

Preheat oven to 400°. Melt butter in a bowl in microwave. Add bread cubes, apples, celery, pecans, salt and pepper. Cut a large pocket in the side of each pork chop; spoon stuffing loosely into pockets. Spray a large baking dish with cooking spray. Place stuffed pork chops in dish. Cover and bake 30 minutes. Uncover and bake 15 minutes longer or until meat juices run clear.

Slow-Roasted Pork Tenderloin

3 tablespoons teriyaki sauce
¼ cup honey
1 teaspoon red pepper flakes
6 garlic cloves, minced
2 (1-pound) pork tenderloins

In a bowl, whisk together teriyaki sauce, honey, red pepper flakes and garlic. Whisk in 1 cup water and add to slow cooker. Add pork; turn to coat. Cook, covered, on low until a thermometer inserted in pork reads 145°, about 7 to 8 hours. Let stand 10 minutes before slicing.

This is a delicious meal that can cook all day while you work. Make your side dishes the night before to reheat at dinnertime and the rest can go in the slow cooker before you leave for work (or better yet, the night before).

This recipe is a winner with my family as well as my guests of farm to table. I make huge batches during the month of October for our fall festivities at the market. It's another easy slow-cooker meal, so what I like to do is prep it the night before and cook it slow and low the next day. It's a quick sandwich dinner too, so it's perfect for the night of baseball, football, soccer, dance, karate, etc. You get the idea! Just wrap the sandwiches in foil to eat on the go.

Sweet & Tangy Pulled Pork

Yield: 8 servings

1 (3- to 4-pound) boneless pork butt
Salt and pepper to taste
2 garlic cloves, minced

BBQ Sauce:
2 cups ketchup
½ cup honey
2 tablespoons Dijon mustard
2 tablespoons brown sugar
1 tablespoon paprika
½ tablespoon garlic powder
½ tablespoon onion powder
Dash cayenne pepper

Place pork butt in slow cooker. Add salt, pepper, garlic and water to cover. Cook on low 8 hours (or 4 hours on high). Remove pork butt from slow cooker and transfer to heat-safe dish. With 2 forks, shred meat. Combine BBQ Sauce ingredients in a saucepan over medium heat; cook, mixing well, just until heated through. Pour sauce over meat and mix well. (May return to slow cooker on warm until ready to serve.) Serve on Kaiser rolls.

BBQ Country Ribs

4 to 6 garlic cloves
2 cups ketchup
½ cup honey
2 tablespoons Dijon mustard
2 tablespoons brown sugar
2 tablespoons Worcestershire sauce
1 lemon, juiced
1 tablespoon paprika
½ tablespoon garlic powder
½ tablespoon onion powder
Dash cayenne pepper
Salt and pepper to taste
2 to 3 pounds country spare ribs

Add all ingredients, except ribs, to slow cooker and whisk to mix well. Add ribs and stir to cover in sauce. Cook on low 7 to 8 hours (or high 3 to 4 hours).

This is a great fall meal if you want to eat them right out of the slow cooker as is. However, stick them on a baking sheet under the open flame of a broiler for a couple minutes and watch the ribs transform into a summer barbecue. Pair them with mac and cheese or potato salad, depending on your preference.

Fun, fun, fun—Asian food at home on a kabob! What kid wouldn't eat that for dinner? I would recommend prepping this the night before, so they can marinate properly. It will also make them really easy to cook and get on the table for dinner on a busy weeknight. Pair with some rice and, boom! Dinner is served.

Asian Pork Kabobs

Yield: 4 servings

¼ cup teriyaki sauce
2 tablespoons honey
1 pound thick, boneless pork chops,
cut into 1-inch cubes
1 medium onion, quartered
1 medium sweet red bell pepper,
cut into 2-inch pieces
1 medium green bell pepper,
cut into 2-inch pieces
1 pineapple, skin removed, cored,
quartered then cut into chunks

Preheat oven to 400°. In a bowl, combine teriyaki sauce and honey. Set aside. On 4 metal (or soaked wooden) skewers, alternately thread pork, onion, red pepper, green pepper and pineapple. Place on baking sheet and drizzle with marinade on both sides. Bake, uncovered, turning occasionally, 10 to 15 minutes, or until vegetables are tender and meat is no longer pink.

Optional: Pour marinade in a large resealable plastic bag; add pork. Seal bag and turn to coat; refrigerate at least 2 hours or overnight for stronger flavor.

This is a very fun meal for the kiddos to eat and an easy meal to make. Growing up, we ate kielbasa for every holiday as an appetizer. It screams holiday to me, so therefore, it feels a little extra special when I prepare it. Now, let's just also agree that anything on a kabob is extra special. Now you're a supermom!

Smoked Kielbasa & Apple Kabobs

Yield: 8 servings

2 pounds smoked kielbasa, cut into 1½-inch pieces
2 medium tart apples, cut into chunks
1 small red onion, quartered
1 medium red bell pepper, cut into 1-inch pieces
1 medium green bell pepper, cut into 1-inch pieces
Olive oil
Sea salt

Preheat oven to 425°. On 8 metal (or soaked wooden) skewers, alternately thread sausage, apple, onion and peppers. Place on baking sheet, brush with olive oil and season to taste with salt. Bake, uncovered, 10 minutes. Flip kabobs and brush with additional olive oil; cook an additional 10 minutes (or 15 minutes for crispier kielbasa). Sprinkle with additional sea salt to taste.

I just love a good breaded pork chop. It's a hearty, down-home, country kind of meal that's easy to make. Throw some potatoes in the oven and open a jar of applesauce for a super simple meal any night of the week.

Breaded Pork Chops

Yield: 6 servings

½ cup milk
1 egg, lightly beaten
6 (1-inch-thick) pork chops
1½ cups breadcrumbs
2 tablespoons olive oil

Preheat oven to 400°. In a bowl, combine milk and egg. Dip each pork chop in the mixture, then coat with breadcrumbs, patting to make a thick coating. Place pork chops in a casserole dish coated with the olive oil. Bake, uncovered, about 15 minutes per side or until browned and no pink remains inside.

Slow-Cooker Pork Chop Cacciatore

Yield: 4 to 6 servings

6 garlic cloves, minced
1 medium green bell pepper, chopped
1 small onion, chopped
4 to 6 (1-inch-thick) boneless pork chops
1 (28-ounce) can crushed tomatoes
½ cup dry white wine
1 cup sliced fresh portobello mushrooms
2 tablespoons chopped fresh parsley
½ cup grated Parmesan cheese
plus more for topping
Salt and pepper to taste

Combine all ingredients in a slow cooker. Cook on low 8 hours (or high 4 hours). Top with additional Parmesan and serve hot.

This is one of my favorite slow cooker recipes when I don't have a lot of time to prep but want a mouth-watering dinner. Everything gets tossed in at one time, and you can even prep it the night before. Keep it in the fridge overnight to cook the next morning before you start your day. The tomatoes and wine cook all day, making a delicious sauce to serve over your favorite pasta.

This one-pan meal can be served over pasta for a quick and complete meal any night of the week. My grandpa used to pick mushrooms in the wild when I was a little girl, and they were so good. The secret is to sauté the mushrooms almost to the point of crispness to bring out their delicious, earthy flavor.

Boneless Pork Chops in Mushroom Sauce

Yield: 4 to 6 servings

4 to 6 (1-inch-thick) boneless pork chops
Salt and pepper to taste
Olive oil
2 cups sliced mushrooms
2 cups sliced onion
4 tablespoons butter, divided
1 tablespoon flour
1 cup dry white wine
2 tablespoons half-and-half

Season pork on both sides. In a pan over medium-high heat, add a drizzle of olive oil. Cook pork chops about 6 to 8 minutes per side until no longer pink. Remove from pan and cover. To same pan, add mushrooms, onion and 2 tablespoons butter. Sauté until mushrooms are brown and crispy on the edges. Stir in flour. Add wine. Cook until sauce thickens, about 3 to 5 minutes. Turn off heat. Stir in remaining 2 tablespoons butter until incorporated; stir in half-and-half. Return pork chops to pan and spoon sauce over them. Serve warm.

Slow-Cooker Italian Porchetta

Yield: 8 servings

2 tablespoons fennel seeds
1 tablespoon coarse sea salt
2 teaspoons fresh ground black pepper
1 teaspoon dried crushed red pepper
6 large garlic cloves, minced
1 (5½- to 6-pound) boneless pork shoulder (Boston butt), excess fat trimmed with thin layer left intact
2 tablespoons extra virgin olive oil plus additional for brushing
1 cup dry white wine (one you like to drink)
½ cup chicken stock

Combine fennel seeds, salt, black pepper and red pepper. Rub garlic all over pork, then coat with spice mixture. In slow cooker, place roast fat side up with coating intact. Add olive oil, wine and chicken stock. Cook 8 hours on low or 4 hours on high, brushing with oil every hour or so to prevent drying out. Transfer pork to cutting board. Let pork rest 15 minutes and slice.

Optional: Loosely cover pork with wax paper and refrigerate overnight before cooking for better flavor.

This is such a savory way to prepare a pork roast. I absolutely love any kind of rub because of the simplicity. It's also such an easy way to prepare any meat, and it really brings out the flavor. The slow cooker is the perfect place for this beauty, and it makes it that much easier for a busy weeknight meal.

Mother—that was the bank where we deposited all our hurts and worries. —T. DeWitt Talmage

I am pretty sure my family could eat seafood all day every day and not ever tire of it. Seafood is one of the easiest things to make and can be made rather quickly. It feels special because I associate it with wonderful holiday or vacation memories. The Fourth of July party my grandma and grandpa Kenosky hosted was all about homemade clam chowder and dozens upon dozens of steamed clams. When we vacation, it's usually to the beach where seafood is fresh and bountiful, so we eat it every night. When the Annual Covington Picnic is happening in our little town, we have steamed clams every night. Christmas Eve was, and still is, about all the lobster tails you can eat.

New Year's Eve? You guessed it, seafood. Date nights and any kind of celebratory family dinner always start with shrimp cocktail. Heck, I even do seafood for Super Bowl Sunday. I don't even watch the game; it's just another excuse to make great food. Now, I'm not telling you to reserve this chapter merely for holidays and vacations; it's actually quite the opposite because I believe every day should be special. One of the best things about seafood for the busy mom is that it can be frozen, so you may purchase it ahead of time. Simply take your seafood out of the freezer to defrost in the fridge the night before, and you'll have dinner ready in minutes. These recipes are easy enough to make on a weeknight so that even a boring Tuesday, when you have the rest of the work week ahead of you, can be extra special with a seafood dinner.

If I whip up Drunkin' Steamers on a weeknight, I guarantee Kaden will ask me what we're celebrating. If I make lobster on a weeknight, he asks if we've hit the Pennsylvania lottery!

F2T Fabulous Tip: Eat outside! Nothing says "we're celebrating a special occasion" like eating outdoors. Whether you eat at a picnic table under a tree, on your patio table by the pool, or on a picnic blanket in the middle of your yard, it instantly makes a regular night a little more special. Take it a step further by adding candles or stringing lights for added sparkle and magic. Always remember that no matter how simple it may seem, you are making a great memory for your children.

Unlike my son who likes them raw, this is how I eat my oysters. My mom used to make these in a deep fryer when we were kids and served them with fries and coleslaw. With the invention of the air fryer, they are not only delicious but a bit healthier. They are super easy to make and can go from fryer to table in minutes. The coleslaw may be made the day before but it's basically like tossing a salad so you can whip it up while your oysters are in the fryer. Dipped in ketchup along with crispy fries is the way I like them best. Be warned, you may want to double, even triple, this recipe.

Crispy Fried Oysters

Yield: 1 dozen

2 large eggs
1 cup dry breadcrumbs
½ teaspoon dill weed
½ teaspoon dried parsley
⅛ teaspoon salt
⅛ teaspoon pepper
½ teaspoon paprika
1 (8-ounce) container whole oysters, drained
Vegetable oil for frying, if using frying pan method

In a shallow bowl, whisk eggs. In a second bowl, combine breadcrumbs, dill, parsley, salt, pepper and paprika. Dip oysters in egg, and coat with crumb mixture. Fry in skillet with hot oil until golden brown, flipping once, about 4 minutes per side (or place in air fryer). Drain on paper towels and serve with a side of ketchup or cocktail sauce.

Fish Nuggets

Yield: 4 to 6 servings

¾ cup seasoned breadcrumbs
Salt and pepper to taste
2 eggs
1 pound Alaskan cod fillets, cut into
1-inch cubes
Butter-flavored cooking spray

In a shallow bowl, whisk together breadcrumbs, salt and pepper; whisk eggs in a separate bowl. Dip fish in egg, then roll in breadcrumbs. Place in air fryer; spray with cooking spray. Cook at 380° for 12 to 15 minutes or to desired crispness.

I realize fish sticks are a typical cliché kid's meal. However, minced fish isn't always fun for us adults. The thought of fish sticks takes me right back to 1970-something, when we had dinner with the sitter so that my parents could actually go out to an adult dinner. Nowadays, I really like the idea of knowing what I'm eating and prefer preparing it from scratch whenever possible. Fish sticks with pierogies is also my husband's favorite meal, so, of course, I had to create my own version for my sweetheart. Serve this one with my Pierogi-Stuffed Shells (page 202) for a complete meal. It's Ian approved!

This is one of my favorite dinners to order out! It's rich and decadent. Fresh scallops say special occasion or vacation to me, which is why I love to get that same feeling from food at home every once in a while. These are super simple to make with very minimal prep time. Add a Twice-Baked Potato (page 190) and a salad to complete this scrumptious meal.

Pan-Seared Sea Scallops

Yield: 4 servings

1 pound sea scallops
2 tablespoons butter
1 tablespoon olive oil
½ teaspoon salt
1 lemon, halved (1 half sliced), optional

Dry scallops on a paper towel, patting to help release moisture. In a large skillet, heat butter and oil over medium-high heat. Add scallops; cook 1½ to 2 minutes on each side or until firm and opaque. Remove from pan; season with salt. Top with a lemon slice for garnish and a squeeze of fresh lemon juice. Serve immediately.

Shrimp Scampi

Yield: 4 servings

3 to 4 garlic cloves, minced
½ stick butter, cubed
2 tablespoons olive oil
2 lemons, juiced
½ cup dry white wine
½ teaspoon pepper
2 cups large cooked shrimp,
  peeled and deveined
¼ cup grated Parmesan cheese
¼ cup minced fresh parsley
Cooked angel hair pasta, optional

In a skillet over medium heat, sauté garlic in butter and oil until tender. Stir in lemon juice, wine and pepper; cook, stirring, 10 to 12 minutes or until sauce thickens slightly. Add shrimp and cook an additional 3 to 4 minutes until heated through. Sprinkle with Parmesan and parsley. May be served over pasta.

Optional: For red sauce, add a 14-ounce can of crushed tomatoes along with the wine.

This scampi was a family favorite when I was a kid. It's also a one-pot meal with the addition of your favorite pasta or rice, which I love. My mom used to make this in both a red and white sauce just to change it up every now and then. I prefer a white sauce because to me, it allows you to get more of the shrimp flavor. However, you can simply add a can of crushed tomatoes, and it instantly becomes an entirely different dish. It's also something you can cook in about 15 to 20 minutes any night of the week with very minimal prep time.

Pan-Seared Simple Salmon

Yield: 4 servings

4 (6-ounce) salmon fillets
Salt and pepper to taste
3 tablespoons olive oil

Season fillets with salt and pepper. In a large skillet over medium-high heat, cook salmon in oil 3 to 4 minutes each side to achieve a good sear. Turn heat off and cover with lid. Let sit until the insides are no longer translucent and the fillets are fully cooked, approximately 5 minutes.

Sometimes it's not necessary to make a recipe difficult. Often, a fresh piece of fish or even a fresh steak speaks for itself with just a little salt and pepper along with a good sear. I make this salmon recipe all the time. It's so easy but tastes like you're out to dinner at a nice restaurant. I like to serve this with a simple Greek salad made with fresh Bibb lettuce from our friends at Pocono Hydrofarm. They produce fresh-grown lettuce all year round. Every once in a while, I'll serve it with some jasmine rice and roasted asparagus if we're really hungry.

Oh, the famous Drunken Steamers. What, you haven't heard of them? Well, they are famous in our family and in Cape May, New Jersey. We take a yearly vacation to Cape May to spend a little quality time together before Kaden heads back to school. I've been going there with my family since I was a baby. It's nostalgic and anyone who's read my books knows how much I love nostalgia. The thing is, Kaden and I have discovered a new side of Cape May together with new adventures. From lighthouse and ghost trolley tours to movies on the beach, it's very special to us. The one thing that is a constant is Harry's Restaurant for dinner. Every. Single. Night! Kaden tried his first Cape May Salt there, which is raw oysters, and fell in love with them. He also loves their Drunken Steamers, which are basically steamed clams in the most amazing broth ever. They're so good he usually orders several dozen. So what do we do the rest of the year when we're not on vacay? Well, we make our own of course. This recipe is pretty close to Harry's, but one of these years, I'm going to just ask them to share their recipe with me.

Our Drunken Steamers

Yield: 2 to 4 servings

Salt and pepper to taste
1 teaspoon crushed red pepper flakes
1 bay leaf
1 teaspoon dried thyme
50 fresh littleneck clams, soaked at least 18 hours in salt water to purge sand
5 garlic cloves, minced
1 small onion, finely chopped
2 tablespoons olive oil
1 cup dry white wine (or chicken stock)

Heat 6 to 8 cups water and seasonings in a large stockpot over high heat. Add clams, cover, and steam until clams open. Remove clams (discarding any that do not open); reserve 3 cups clam stock. In a skillet over medium heat, sauté garlic and onion in oil until tender, about 4 minutes. Add reserved clam stock and wine. Bring to a boil and cook, uncovered, 25 to 30 minutes to reduce sauce. Pour sauce over clams and serve with crusty bread..

Baked Tilapia with Capers

Yield: 4 servings

4 (6-ounce) tilapia fillets
4 tablespoons butter, melted
Salt and pepper to taste
¼ teaspoon paprika
2 tablespoons drained capers
1 lemon, halved

Place tilapia in an ungreased 9x13-inch baking dish. Top each fillet with 1 tablespoon butter. Sprinkle salt, pepper, paprika and capers on each. Bake, uncovered, at 425° for 10 to 15 minutes or until fish flakes easily with a fork. Squeeze juice from half the lemon over fish; slice remaining half to use as a garnish.

Tilapia is mild in flavor and slightly meaty. It's also super simple to prepare and cooks in minutes. You will have this meal from prep to table in 15 minutes tops. The capers make it a little extra special too. Serve it with a side of rice and a salad for a quick, complete weeknight meal. You can always make a big batch of rice ahead of time to stick in the fridge, then just heat throughout the week to accompany any meal.

What's better than a one-pot meal? One that looks like you've worked for hours to create. This is one of those meals! It has your protein, starch, and veggies all in one. Oh, and did I mention it's delicious and a little fancy? We love our seafood but if your kiddos aren't too fond of it, simply substitute chicken for the shrimp. It's just as good. Serve with penne pasta for a deliciously complete and satisfying meal.

Shrimp & Asparagus

Yield: 4 servings

1 pound fresh asparagus, trimmed and cut into 1-inch pieces
½ cup finely chopped onions
2 tablespoons butter
2 cups cooked large shrimp, peeled and deveined
Salt and pepper
2 teaspoons all-purpose flour
½ cup half-and-half
½ cup grated Parmesan cheese, divided
2 cups cooked penne pasta, optional

In a large nonstick skillet over medium heat, sauté asparagus and onion in butter 4 minutes. Add shrimp; cook and stir 3 minutes or until shrimp are heated. Add salt and pepper to taste. Remove and keep warm. In a small bowl, combine flour and half-and-half until smooth; gradually add to the skillet. Bring to a boil; cook and stir about 2 minutes or until thickened. Stir in ¼ cup cheese. Remove from the heat. Toss pasta with shrimp mixture, then add sauce. Sprinkle with remaining cheese.

Often, I'm really just in the mood for a simple white fish. You can purchase it ahead of time, pop it in the freezer, and take it out to defrost in your fridge the night before. It literally takes six minutes to cook with an additional three minutes (maybe) of prep, making it a great weeknight meal. The Cajun seasoning in this recipe takes this simple fish to another level. Make sure you air out the kitchen though. This fish will definitely be blackened in every sense of the word. You can smell the heat! Serve with a simple salad or my Sautéed Zucchini with Sun-Dried Tomato (page 191) to balance the heat and cool your taste buds.

Blackened Catfish

Yield: 4 servings

2 teaspoons salt
2 teaspoons garlic powder
2 teaspoons paprika
1 teaspoon ground black pepper
1 teaspoon onion powder
1 teaspoon cayenne pepper
1 teaspoon dried oregano
1 teaspoon dried thyme
½ teaspoon red pepper flakes, optional
4 catfish fillets (about 1 pound)
1 tablespoon butter
1 lemon

Combine spices in a small, flat bowl. Dredge catfish fillets until evenly coated on both sides. Heat skillet on high until very hot. Melt butter in pan. Add fish and cook approximately 3 minutes per side or until fish flakes easily with a fork. Squeeze lemon over fish and serve.

Crab Cakes

1 pound fresh lump crabmeat
1½ cups breadcrumbs
1 large egg, beaten
2 tablespoons mayonnaise
⅓ cup chopped celery
⅓ cup chopped onion
1 tablespoon Old Bay seasoning
2 tablespoons minced fresh parsley
Juice from ½ lemon
1 teaspoon Dijon mustard
Salt and pepper to taste
2 to 4 tablespoons vegetable oil, optional

In a large bowl, combine all ingredients, except oil. Shape into 8 patties. Broil patties or cook in a skillet in oil 4 minutes on each side or until golden brown. Tip: Let them get nice and brown before flipping, so they don't fall apart. Drain on a paper towel and serve hot. Busy mom freeze option: Freeze cooled crab cakes in freezer containers or large zip-close plastic bags (lay flat), separating layers with wax paper. To use, reheat crab cakes on a baking sheet in a 325° oven until heated through.

This recipe will soon become one of your faves whether you serve it on a bed of mixed greens with olive oil and a squeeze of lemon or on a hard roll with lettuce and tartar sauce. You may also serve it as an appetizer. I've even included a freeze option so you can get a couple nights out of this dinner.

Perfect Shrimp Cocktail

Shrimp:

1 pound fresh colossal wild-caught shrimp
(about 16 shrimp)

Cocktail Sauce:

2 tablespoons horseradish
¾ cup ketchup
1 lemon, halved

Rub:

1 tablespoon Old Bay seasoning
¼ teaspoon sea salt
¼ teaspoon all-purpose seasoning

Bring 6 cups water to a boil in a stockpot over high heat. Add shrimp and cook until pink, about 6 minutes. Drain and let cool. Peel and devein under cold water leaving tails attached. In a bowl, mix horseradish, ketchup and juice of half a lemon. Set aside. In a separate bowl, combine Old Bay, salt and all-purpose seasoning; mix. Roll shrimp from front to back (basically, where the shrimp was deveined) in the mixture. Wedge remaining lemon. Serve shrimp chilled with lemon wedges and Cocktail Sauce.

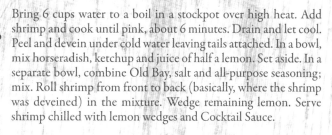

Shrimp Cocktail may be simple but only if it's done right. Serve this in half an avocado on top of my delicious steak salad, and it's an instant "surf and turf" meal complete with veggies!

Did you knoww, when kids go to bed, you can hear yourself think again. I sound fabulous. —Paige Kellerman

Growing up on a farm in the '70s, gardens were a way of life. Both sets of grandparents had a garden and so did my parents. When my sister and I were little, we'd pick veggies in Grandma's garden for what felt like hours. Grandma had such a green thumb that everything she grew was incredibly abundant. The green beans seemed to go on for days. My favorite veggies to pick were cucumbers and peas because we would eat them right off the vines. All the flavors of summer came from the garden. The cucumbers and fresh dill we picked would become the best pickles I'd ever tasted. Because it would take some time for the pickles to be ready once canned, Grandma always made a big pot of crock-dill pickles. In her kitchen, she would sit the big crock on a chair, then cover it with a dish towel topped with a kitchen plate. Oh, how I loved to peek under that towel and grab a pickle, ready or not. They were so delicious.

Grandma Storm lived on the farm next door and sold produce and fresh eggs for a living. Some of the freshest vegetables in our little town of Daleville came from Farmer Storm's stand. Anyone who grew up here remembers my grandparents. My sister and I played behind the counter while Grandma worked, and Grandpa was in the field or tending his chickens. The one thing they always stopped working for was lunch, as they had breakfast and supper at home. Each day at noon, Grandpa would come over to the market to have lunch with Grandma. They knew how to celebrate life's little moments and to praise each day by eating together as a family. They were best friends, and it kept their marriage and their family strong.

We're all busy. Trust me, I get it. It's not easy to find time for those little moments, but we should try. Even if it's a foil-covered dinner left on the stove for your kids to reheat, your family will remember the effort you put forth for them. Maybe it's even takeout served on real dinner plates, but that's okay, too. The truth is that food equals love. When you're little, it makes you feel happy, fulfilled, and loved. It also creates special memories to pass down through generations when you're all grown up. In addition to being a mother and wife, cooking gives me a purpose. When I'm in the kitchen, I'm creating something to make people happy. It's also a project that you can accomplish start to finish in under an hour. I can't even do laundry that fast, not to mention that laundry isn't all that fulfilling. Anyhoo, eat your vegetables. That's both the theme of this chapter and the words your children will never forget.

F2T Fabulous Tip: Turn your dining room or kitchen into a restaurant and let the kiddos help serve. Plan the menu the day or weekend before, and let the kids make menus as an art project. Serve dinner in courses, rather than family style, like you would enjoy while dining out complete with bread for the table. How fun to pretend you're out while eating in. Take it a step further by letting the kids wash the dishes! A little extra work never hurt anyone and if you cooked, it's only fair that they serve and clean. Everyone needs a role to play in your restaurant.

With the invention of the air fryer, it's easier than ever to make your own homemade fries. These are officially kid-tested and Kaden-approved. He says they're the best fries he's ever had so it's a win. They are much more cost effective (and healthier) than frozen, so it's a win-win.

Seasoned French Fries

Yield: 4 to 6 servings

4 potatoes, peeled and cut into shoestrings
2 tablespoons olive oil
1 tablespoon all-purpose seasoning
Salt and pepper to taste

In a bowl, toss potatoes in olive oil and seasonings until evenly coated. Cook at 400° in air fryer 25 minutes, tossing once.

Cinnamon-Sugar Sweet Potato Fries

Yield: 4 to 6 servings

4 sweet potatoes, peeled and cut into shoe-strings
2 tablespoons olive oil
1 teaspoon ground cinnamon
1 tablespoon sugar

In a bowl, toss potatoes in olive oil, cinnamon and sugar until evenly coated. Cook at 400° in air fryer for 25 minutes, tossing once.

One of my favorite ways to eat a simple piece of toast when I was a little girl was with cinnamon and sugar. Who am I kidding? I still eat it that way. It's the perfect combination of flavors. I mean, they even made it into a cereal so I can't be wrong about this one. Add cinnamon and sugar to your sweet potato fries for a little extra sweetness just in case your kiddos aren't sweet enough. These fries are a great compliment to chicken nuggets with a side of barbecue sauce for dipping.

Scalloped Potatoes

Yield: 4 servings

3 tablespoons all-purpose flour
2 cups milk
4 tablespoons melted butter, divided
¼ teaspoon salt
Dash pepper
¾ cup shredded Cheddar cheese
4 cups peeled and thinly sliced potatoes
(about 4 medium)
1 cup thinly sliced red onion
4 garlic cloves, minced
½ cup soft breadcrumbs (or toast 3 slices
bread and crumble)
Parsley flakes for garnish

In a saucepan, combine flour, milk, 2 tablespoons butter, salt and pepper, whisking until smooth. Slowly bring to a boil. Cook, stirring, 1 to 2 minutes or until thickened. Add cheese and stir until melted; remove from heat. In a greased 9x12-inch baking dish, layer half the potatoes, onion, garlic and white sauce. Repeat layers. Toss breadcrumbs in remaining butter; sprinkle over top. Cover and bake at 375° for 50 to 55 minutes or until potatoes are tender. Increase heat to 425° and bake, uncovered, an additional 15 to 20 minutes until golden brown. Garnish with parsley.

This one may take a little extra effort, but if my mom could do it on a work night, we can do it too. The trick is to make it up the night before so you can either bake it fully when you get home or just heat it up. This was one of my faves as a kid. Mom made the most delicious candied ham. And what was sitting in the casserole dish right next to it to be reheated for dinner? You guessed it, creamy scalloped potatoes.

One of the easiest, most nutritious ways to eat your veggies is to roast them. All the nutrients stay put; they don't get boiled out. It's also the tastiest in my opinion. Kaden says, "Mom, do you know any other kids that ask for broccoli for dinner?" I think I am pretty lucky that my kiddo likes his veggies but honestly, I do think it's all about how you make them. To me, there's nothing worse than having a beautiful dinner with a boiled slab of veggies on your plate. Frozen veggies are one thing but if you're preparing something fresh, roast those babies! It's well worth it and super simple.

Roasted Veggies

Yield: 4 to 6 servings

3 heads broccoli, cut into florets
2 cups whole baby carrots
4 small potatoes, sliced
1 pint grape tomatoes
8 to 10 garlic cloves
4 tablespoons olive oil, divided
Salt and pepper to taste

Preheat oven to 400°. Place vegetables and garlic on a large baking sheet; toss with 2 tablespoons oil. Sprinkle with salt and pepper. Roast until tender, 20 to 25 minutes, stirring occasionally. Transfer to a large bowl. Drizzle with remaining 2 tablespoons oil.

Glazed carrots have always been one of my favorite side dishes to round out a meal. This recipe is sweet and savory which is always a winner in our family.

Glazed Carrots

Yield: 4 servings

3 cups fresh baby carrots
4 tablespoons butter
2 tablespoon brown sugar
1 teaspoon Dijon mustard
Salt and pepper to taste

In a medium pot, bring 1½ cups water and carrots to a boil. Cook 12 to 15 minutes until tender when pierced with fork; drain. Return to medium-high heat. Add butter, brown sugar, mustard, salt and pepper. Cook and stir 1 minute until the sugar is dissolved and sauce is bubbly. Stir to coat carrots with glaze.

Roasted Kale & Cherry Tomatoes

Yield: 4 servings

2 bunches (6 to 8 cups) kale, washed
1 pint grape tomatoes
2 tablespoons olive oil
Sea salt, to taste
Pepper to taste

Preheat oven to 400°. Remove tough stems from kale and tear leaves into large pieces. Place kale and tomatoes on a large baking sheet and toss with olive oil, salt and pepper. Bake, uncovered, until crisp and just starting to brown, about 15 minutes. Toss once. Let stand at least 5 minutes before serving.

This quick and simple side dish is packed full of nutrients. Here's a secret, the kiddos will eat the kale like potato chips if you make them crispy enough and with a little sprinkle of salt. I also like to replace pasta with kale on occasion because it's not so heavy. I can't get enough leafy greens in my life.

Sautéed Spinach & Garlic

Yield: 4 servings

6 garlic cloves, roughly chopped
2 tablespoons olive oil
½ cup white wine or chicken broth
6 cups tightly packed fresh baby spinach
Salt to taste

In a large skillet, sauté garlic in oil 1 minute. Add wine. Bring to a boil; cook until liquid is reduced by half. Add spinach and salt. Stir while cooking 2 minutes or just until spinach is wilted.

My child loves his spinach. I've been very lucky with Kaden when it comes to his veggies. Even when he was very young, Kaden would eat spinach by the fistful. This is such a healthy, yet easy, way to get your leafy greens. The garlic makes it extra flavorful and delicious.

I could write a whole book on my love for squash blossoms and memories of my Italian grandmother. I'll try to make this short. My grandmother had the most amazing garden ever. My sister and I spent plenty of time either picking veggies or weeding so I know firsthand. Grandmother would do almost anything to protect it including leaning out her bedroom window with a BB gun aiming at anything (not human) that would try to take a nibble. Out of all the veggies she would prepare, these squash flowers were my favorite. She would say, "pick them in the morning before they close because the bumble bees like to hide in them," and she was right, that's the general rule. You'll probably want to grow your own though, they're hard to find in the store and you can never eat just one.

Fried Squash Blossoms

Yield: 4 servings

2 tablespoons all-purpose flour
½ teaspoon baking powder
2 eggs
1 tablespoon water
Salt and pepper to taste
Vegetable oil for frying
12 large freshly picked squash blossoms

In a medium bowl, combine first 5 ingredients and stir until smooth. In a skillet, heat 2 inches oil to 375°. Dip blossoms into batter and fry in oil a few at a time until crisp on both sides. Drain on paper towels. Keep warm until serving.

Southern Baked Beans

2 (28-ounce) cans baked beans
1 green bell pepper, chopped
1 red bell pepper, chopped
1 medium onion, chopped
1 tablespoon vegetable oil
½ pound sliced bacon, cooked and crumbled
1 cup packed brown sugar

Drain beans and set aside. In a cast-iron skillet, sauté peppers and onion in oil until tender. Add beans and remaining ingredients. Stir until blended. Bake, uncovered, at 350° for 30 to 45 minutes or until heated through.

This was always one of my mother's favorite side dishes and one of her go-to dishes when asked to bring something to a party. What's a barbecue dinner without beans after all? This sweet and savory recipe is one of my favorites.

There's no quick way to make risotto folks; sorry. It's a time-consuming dish. However, it's pretty easy to make and is so hearty I can serve it as a main dish. This creamy mushroom risotto is one of my favorites on a cold winter day. It's worth the extra effort and if you come from a big Italian family, a staple.

Mushroom Risotto

Yield: 6 servings

1½ cups water
1 (14-ounce) can reduced-sodium beef broth
½ cup chopped shallots
2 garlic cloves, minced
1 tablespoon canola oil
1 cup uncooked arborio rice
1 tablespoon minced fresh thyme
(or 1 teaspoon dried)
½ teaspoon salt
½ teaspoon pepper
½ cup white wine or additional
reduced-sodium beef broth
1 cup chopped baby
portobello mushrooms
¼ cup grated Parmesan cheese
Mascarpone for garnish, optional

In a large saucepan, heat water and broth and keep warm. In a large saucepan, sauté shallots and garlic in oil 2 to 3 minutes or until shallots are tender. Add rice, thyme, salt and pepper; cook and stir 2 to 3 minutes. Reduce heat; stir in wine. Cook and stir until all liquid is absorbed. Add heated broth, ½ cup at a time, stirring constantly. Allow liquid to absorb between additions. Cook just until risotto is creamy and rice is almost tender. (Cooking time is about 20 minutes.)Add mushrooms and Parmesan; stir gently until cheese is melted. Garnish each serving with a heaping tablespoon of mascarpone. Serve immediately. Freeze option: Before adding mascarpone cheese, freeze cooled risotto mixture in freezer containers. To use, partially thaw in refrigerator overnight. Heat through in a saucepan, stirring occasionally and adding a little broth or water if necessary. Garnish as directed.

Cauliflower-Garlic Mash

1 large head cauliflower, cut into florets
1 whole garlic bulb
1 teaspoon olive oil
4 tablespoons milk
3 tablespoons butter
¼ cup grated Parmesan cheese
Salt and pepper to taste
½ teaspoon parsley
Cracked black pepper and minced fresh chives, optional

Place 1 inch water in a large saucepan over medium-high heat; add cauliflower. While cauliflower cooks, prepare roasted garlic. Using a sharp knife, cut about ¼ inch from top of garlic bulb, exposing the individual cloves. Drizzle with 1 teaspoon olive oil, cover with foil and roast in preheated 400° oven about 15 minutes. After cauliflower comes to a boil, reduce heat. Simmer, covered, until tender, 10 to 15 minutes, stirring occasionally. Drain cauliflower; return to pan. Squeeze garlic from bulb into cauliflower. Mash cauliflower mixture to desired consistency. Stir in milk, butter, Parmesan, salt and pepper and parsley. If desired, sprinkle with cracked pepper or chives.

This is a nice substitute for potatoes if you're looking to switch things up a bit, and they're so tasty. It's also a carb-free option--bonus!

Not only is roasting your veggies one of the best ways to get the most nutrition from them, they are also so nice and crispy it's one of the best ways to get children to eat them. They are so flavorful.

Roasted Brussels Sprouts

Yield: 4 to 6 servings

1½ pounds fresh Brussels sprouts, trimmed and halved

2 tablespoons plus 1 teaspoon truffle oil, divided

½ teaspoon salt

¼ teaspoon pepper

In a large bowl, drizzle Brussels sprouts with 1 tablespoon truffle oil; toss to coat. Transfer to a baking sheet. Bake, uncovered, at 400° for 15 to 20 minutes or until tender and golden brown, tossing occasionally. Transfer to a serving bowl; sprinkle with salt and pepper, drizzle with remaining oil.

Cheesy Stuffed Zucchini

Yield: 4 servings

2 medium zucchini
1 small tomato, chopped
2 tablespoons finely chopped red onion
2 tablespoons butter
½ cup panko breadcrumbs
Salt and pepper to taste
2 tablespoons chopped fresh parsley
2 tablespoons grated Parmesan cheese
½ cup shredded mozzarella cheese

Cut zucchini in half lengthwise. Scoop out pulp, leaving a ¼-in. shell. Chop pulp; set shells aside. In a nonstick skillet, saute the zucchini pulp and onion in butter 5 to 7 minutes or until tender. Stir in breadcrumbs, salt, pepper, Parmesan, parsley and tomato. Place zucchini shells in a baking dish. Fill shells with mixture. Sprinkle with mozzarella, divided evenly. Bake at 400° for 30 to 40 minutes or until lightly browned. Garnish with fresh parsley.

The one vegetable that is very plentiful here in the Northeast in the summertime is zucchini. They're very hearty. They can be stuffed with just about anything but this is one of Kaden's favorite ways so it's kid-tested and approved! This recipe is filling enough for dinner. However, you may also add some cooked ground beef, chicken, turkey or sausage to the recipe and make it a complete meal!

Yes, it's right out of the movie. This is my mom's favorite summertime indulgence, probably because she grows the best tomatoes around. Also, have I mentioned how much I like anything fried? These can double as an appetizer or a side dish. Either way, it's definitely a special summertime treat.

Mom's Fried Green Tomatoes

Yield: 6 servings

1 tablespoon raw sugar
1 cup all-purpose flour
4 to 6 medium green tomatoes,
sliced ½-inch thick
1 tablespoon vegetable oil

Combine sugar and flour; place on a shallow plate. Dredge both sides of each tomato slice in mixture. In a skillet, heat vegetable oil over medium high. Fry tomatoes until brown on both sides but firm enough to hold their shape.

Cabbage & Noodles

8 tablespoons (1 stick) **butter**
1 medium **onion, chopped**
1 small head **cabbage, thinly sliced**
¼ teaspoon **salt**
Dash pepper
2 cups (8 ounces) wide egg
noodles, cooked and drained

Melt butter in a large skillet. Add onion and cook until translucent, about 2 minutes. Add cabbage, cover and cook on low 20 minutes or until cabbage is tender, stirring occasionally. Stir in salt, pepper and noodles. Heat through.

This is the very first dish I ever made for our farm-to-table department at the market, before the department ever existed really. I stood in the market on a Sunday, after cooking the day before, and handed out samples. It's how the whole farm-to-table thing began. That day, I met some of the nicest people as they tasted my samples, and they've supported me ever since. This is a super simple dish that can be made in a big batch, in minutes, for an easy weeknight meal.

These potatoes are so nice; I bake them twice. It's an easy recipe and a step up from the usual mashed potatoes. It's also very versatile. You may add virtually anything you would find at a potato bar for more flavor.

Twice-Baked Potatoes

Yield: 4 to 6 servings

5 potatoes, baked about 40 minutes until tender, and then halved
¼ cup milk
2 tablespoons butter
1 tablespoon chopped chives
¼ cup grated Parmesan cheese
Salt and pepper to taste
Paprika to taste

Remove potato flesh from skins, gently, and place in a bowl. Reserve skins, discarding 1. Add remaining ingredients, except paprika, to bowl and mash until smooth. Distribute mixture between 4 potato skins, sprinkle with paprika and bake in a 400° oven about 15 minutes until golden brown.

Sautéed Zucchini with Sun-Dried Tomatoes

1 tablespoon butter
2 tablespoons olive oil
1 cup sun-dried tomato strips
2 medium zucchini, sliced ½ inch thick
Salt and pepper

Melt butter in a saucepan over medium heat; add oil and sun-dried tomatoes. Toss to coat evenly. Add zucchini and sauté until softened, about 15 to 20 minutes. Season to taste with salt and pepper.

I absolutely love a light, easy dish in the summer or any time of year really. Although, We always have an abundance of zucchini in the summertime so it's a no-brainer. The sun-dried tomatoes add a little interest and extra flavor to a very simple dish.

Roasted veggies is farm to table at its finest. This side dish is my favorite on a chilly autumn day alongside a pot roast or roasted chicken. The sweetness will balance any savory protein for the perfect comforting meal.

Oven-Roasted Carrots

Yield: 4 to 6 servings

8 to 10 carrots, peeled and sliced
in half lengthwise
3 tablespoons brown sugar
2 tablespoons butter

Place carrots on a baking sheet. Toss in brown sugar and dot with butter. Bake in a 400° oven about 20 minutes until softened and golden brown, turning once.

Crispy Herb-Roasted Potatoes

1 teaspoon dried rosemary
1 teaspoon all-purpose seasoning
1 teaspoon onion powder
1 teaspoon garlic powder
1 teaspoon paprika
1 teaspoon dried parsley
Salt and pepper taste
6 potatoes, cubed
2 tablespoons olive oil

Place herbs and spices in a large bowl. Add potatoes and oil. Toss until evenly coated. Bake in a 400° oven 30 to 45 minutes or until golden brown and crispy, tossing once.

This dish is not only super simple, but one you'll make time and time again for it's versatility. You can even eat it for breakfast! You will most likely always have these ingredients on hand as well so no last-minute trips to the grocery store. These potatoes are one of my favorite sides to accompany my Grilled Marinated Italian Chicken, just like Grandma used to make. Now all you need is a salad and dinner is served.

We seasonal folks love the fall. This dish has all my favorite flavors and colors of the season. Enjoy with my slow-cooker pork tenderloin and it will be the perfect combination of comfort foods on a chilly autumn day.

Butternut Squash & Maple Mash

Yield: 4 servings

1 large butternut squash
1 tablespoon pure maple syrup
2 tablespoons butter
Dash cinnamon and nutmeg

Place squash in microwave-safe dish and cook on high 10 minutes. Turn and cook an additional 8 minutes. Place on cutting board and cut off outer skin. Cut in half and scoop out seeds. Discard. Cut flesh into cubes and place in bowl. Add maple syrup and butter; mash until semi-smooth. Sprinkle with cinnamon and nutmeg.

You may not have candy for breakfast, now finish your Pop Tart. —Laney Griner

I have learned so much since we've started farm-to-table meals in our markets. One thing is that not everyone eats meat. When having dinner guests, I like to make everyone feel equally comfortable and satisfied. I will not be the host who treats vegetarian dishes as an afterthought or suggests my vegetarian friends just eat all salads and sides.

At home, I'm lucky to have a veggie-lovin' kid so I don't have to sneak veggies into recipes. However, if your kiddos resist eating their veggies, you'll find some recipes in this chapter they'll enjoy while never knowing they're eating something nutritious. The thing is though, if I'm being honest, just because a recipe contains veggies doesn't necessarily mean its "local" or super healthy. Some recipes here are very healthy. Many of the dishes in this chapter, however, contain quite a lot of cheese and sauce.

Many of these dishes work for guests or family dinner with mixed company by giving meat eaters meatballs or sausage on the side. In this way, they have the option of adding a little something extra to their dish. One of my favorite meals as a little girl was my mom's pierogi lasagna. It literally tastes like a pierogi with all the heartiness of a lasagna. It makes a delicious family dinner but is also sit-down-dinner-with-invited-company worthy.

I love learning something new especially when it comes to food and that comes with pushing myself out of my comfort zone to some degree. What I discovered along the way with this chapter is what I thought would be a light chapter of veggie-only dishes really turned into a chapter of scrumptious comfort foods that are full of flavor. From vegetable lasagna with homemade sauce to stuffed peppers and tomatoes, this chapter will have you excited for leftovers. I hope you enjoy this journey into the world of all things vegetarian. I certainly enjoyed the journey, as did my taste-testing family including our dog Morgan, who I also learned loves zucchini.

F2T Fabulous Tip: It's no secret that Ian and I love our lip-sync battles, and if you've read my last book, you know entertainment by "the cousins" always followed dinner at Grandma and Grandpa's house when I was growing up. Why not turn your dining room into a dinner theatre by letting your kiddos showcase their talent over dessert? Be careful, parents. If you're asking them to perform, you had better have something in your back pocket as well. May I suggest a lip-sync battle?

Pierogi Lasagna

Yield: 8 to 10 servings

4 to 5 medium potatoes, peeled and quartered
1½ sticks butter, divided
½ cup whole milk
Salt and pepper to taste
4 cups shredded sharp Cheddar cheese, divided
1 medium onion, chopped
9 to 12 oven-ready lasagna noodles
1 cup ricotta cheese, divided

Cook potatoes in salted water to cover until soft, about 20 minutes. Drain and place in a large bowl with ½ stick butter and milk. Mash potatoes and season to taste with salt and pepper. Stir in 2 cups Cheddar cheese and set aside. Meanwhile, in a skillet over medium-high heat, sauté onion in remaining 1 stick butter. Treat a 9x13-inch baking dish with nonstick spray 000and layer with a third of the cooked onion and butter. Top with 3 or 4 lasagna noodles and half the potato mixture. Dot with ½ cup ricotta cheese (evenly spaced); season to taste. Repeat layers. Top with 3 or 4 noodles and remaining onion and butter. Bake, covered, at 400° for 45 minutes. Sprinkle with remaining Cheddar cheese and bake, uncovered, an additional 5 minutes or until golden brown. Let stand 5 minutes before serving.

This recipe from my Mom is one of my favorites. It's like a pierogi in a lasagna. It's nice that you can prep it a day ahead or even complete it the day before and reheat. Because pierogis are one of Ian's favorite foods, this Pierogi Lasagna is just one more way I have to his heart.

Homemade pierogies are a labor of love. It's way easier to pick up a box of pierogies from the market, throw them in the microwave, and be done. This version is equally as satisfying as scratch yet pretty darn simple and it's still homemade. You can even make extra, freeze them on a floured tray, portion them in freezer bags, then pull them out of the freezer to heat in the oven for future dinners.

Pierogi-Stuffed Shells

Yield: 4 to 6 servings

**4 medium potatoes, peeled and cubed
24 unbroken pasta shells
1 small onion, sliced
1 stick plus 2 tablespoons butter, divided
½ cup milk
1 teaspoon onion powder
2 cups shredded sharp Cheddar cheese
Salt and pepper**

Place potatoes in a large pot and cover with water. Bring to a boil over high heat. Reduce heat; cover and simmer approximately 20 minutes or until tender. While potatoes are cooking, cook shells per package directions; drain and set aside. Meanwhile, in a large skillet over medium-high heat, sautée onion in 2 tablespoons butter until tender; set aside. In a bowl, mash potatoes with milk, onion powder, cheese and remaining 1 stick butter. Season to taste with salt and pepper. Fill each shell with mixture and place in a 9x13-inch casserole dish. Pour sautéed onions and butter mixture over shells. Serve immediately or place under broiler to brown.

Shells Stuffed with Fresh Spinach & Ricotta

Yield: 8 to 12 servings

1 (12-ounce) box jumbo pasta shells
1 large egg
1 (32-ounce) container ricotta cheese
2 cups tightly packed chopped fresh spinach
Salt and pepper to taste
2 cups grated Parmesan cheese, divided
2 cups shredded mozzarella cheese, divided
3 to 4 cups spaghetti sauce

Preheat oven to 375°. Cook pasta shells according to package directions. Drain; rinse with cold water. In a large bowl, combine egg, ricotta cheese, spinach, salt and pepper. Stir in 1½ cups each cheese. Spread 2 cups sauce in a 9x13-inch baking dish. Fill pasta shells with cheese mixture; place in baking dish. Pour remaining sauce over top. Bake, covered, 40 to 45 minutes or until heated through. Uncover; sprinkle with remaining cheeses. Bake 5 minutes longer or until cheeses are melted. Let stand 5 minutes before serving.

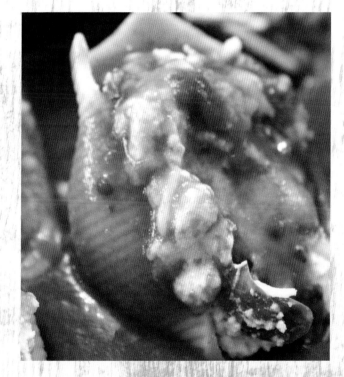

Now this is a way to get your kiddos to eat their veggies, my friends. I mean who doesn't like something smothered in sauce and cheese? They'll never know you've added spinach, trust me, it's that good. If you enjoy meat, this goes beautifully with my mom's homemade sauce and meatball recipe.

Should someone miss out on barbecue just because they don't eat meat?
Can you even imagine a world without barbecue? Me neither.

Barbecue Tofu Kabobs

Yield: 4 servings

1 (16-ounce) package extra-firm tofu,
cut into 8 equal squares
Salt and pepper
1 cup barbecue sauce
1 apple, quartered
1 zucchini, cut into 1-inch-thick slices
8 cherry tomatoes
1 tablespoon olive oil

Preheat oven to broil. Sprinkle tofu pieces with salt and pepper; toss in barbecue sauce. Cut each quartered apple slice in half. Toss apples and remaining veggies in olive oil. Thread 4 skewers with tofu and vegetables in no particular order. Place on baking sheet and broil 8 minutes, turning once.

Portobello-Stuffed Peppers

Yield: 4 servings

4 to 6 small sweet red bell peppers
2 eggs
3 cups chopped mushrooms
½ cup chopped onion
2 cups tomato sauce, divided
½ cup grated Parmesan cheese (3 tablespoons reserved)
½ cup seasoned breadcrumbs
2 tablespoons chopped fresh parsley

Cut and discard tops from peppers; remove seeds. In a bowl, combine eggs, mushrooms, onion and breadcrumbs. Mix together, mashing mushrooms lightly. Spoon mixture into peppers. Sprinkle with reserved 3 tablespoons Parmesan.. Place half the sauce then peppers in slow cooker. Cover with remaining sauce. Cook on high 3 to 4 hours or on low 6 to 7 hours.

I made this one for a farm-to-table dinner when our vegetarian friends were coming to join us. We always have plenty to eat when it comes to a five-course meal but I would never expect someone to "eat around" the meat if they're coming to dinner. This recipe is something I came up with when I was trying to think what was "meaty" enough to stuff a pepper with and that is how this recipe was created. It's now one of my mom's favorite dinners as well.

This is a fun recipe to involve the kiddos. It's full of flavor and everything you need for a complete meal. Of course, it's always nice to add a simple salad and crusty bread if you've worked up an appetite after a busy day.

Parmesan-Stuffed Tomatoes

Yield: 4 to 6 servings

6 medium tomatoes
¾ cup chopped onion
1 (15-ounce) can black beans, drained
8 tablespoons panko breadcrumbs
8 tablespoons shredded
Parmesan cheese, divided
2 tablespoons chopped fresh parsley
2 teaspoons onion powder
2 tablespoons olive oil
4 tablespoons shredded
mozzarella cheese

Cut a thin slice off the top of each tomato. Leaving a ½-inch-thick shell, scoop out the pulp. Invert tomatoes onto paper towels to drain. Chop pulp and place in a bowl. Add onion, beans, breadcrumbs, 4 tablespoons Parmesan and parsley. Spoon about ⅔ cup into each tomato. Place in an ungreased 9x13-inch baking dish. Place tomato tops; cover and bake at 400° for 30 minutes. Sprinkle 1 tablespoon Parmesan and 1 tablespoon mozzarella over each tomato. Bake an additional 15 minutes, uncovered.

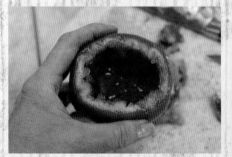

Vegetable Lasagna

Yield: 9 servings

6 to 8 cups spaghetti sauce
1 (16-ounce) carton ricotta cheese
1 egg
1½ cups grated Parmesan cheese, divided
4 cups shredded mozzarella cheese, divided
1 cup roughly chopped fresh spinach
2 small zucchini, cut lengthwise into ¼-inch-thick slices
2 cups shredded carrots
9 to 12 oven-ready lasagna noodles

Preheat oven to 350°. Coat a 9x13-inch casserole dish with cooking spray. Line bottom with enough sauce to cover. In a large bowl, combine ricotta, egg, ½ cup Parmesan, 1 cup mozzarella cheese and spinach. Layer 3 lasagna noodles over sauce in baking dish. Top with 6 tablespoons ricotta mixture evenly spaced plus half the zucchini, half the carrots, 2 cups sauce and 1 cup mozzarella. Repeat layers. Top with the remaining noodles, sauce and cheeses. Cover and bake 40 minutes. Uncover and bake 5 to 10 minutes longer or until edges are bubbly and cheese is slightly browned. Let stand 10 minutes before cutting.

Lasagna on any level, whether it's meat, cheese, veggie or potato, is a great comfort food. What I love is you can prep it days before then pop it in the oven when you're ready. I'm all about working ahead and as a working mom, this is one of those "worth the effort" dishes that can be prepped ahead of time.

This is a great stuffed pepper recipe for non-meat lovers. It's also so fresh and pretty. Nothing takes away the stress of a busy day like knowing dinner is ready in the slow cooker. Add some biscuits, rolls or bread and butter because there's plenty of sauce for dipping!

Slow-Cooker Stuffed Bell Peppers

Yield: 4 servings

4 large green or sweet red bell peppers
2 cups cooked brown rice
½ cup chopped onion
4 tablespoons chopped fresh parsley
Salt and pepper to taste
1 (15-ounce) can black beans,
drained and rinsed
1 egg
2 to 3 cups spaghetti sauce

Cut tops off peppers and remove seeds; set aside. In a large bowl, combine the rice, onion, parsley, salt, pepper, beans and egg; spoon into peppers. Transfer to slow cooker. Pour sauce over peppers. Cover and cook on low 6 to 8 hours or on high 3 to 4 hours.

Angel Hair Pasta with Sun-Dried Tomatoes

Yield: 6 servings

6 tablespoons extra virgin olive oil
6 to 8 fresh garlic cloves, chopped
½ cup finely chopped sun-dried tomatoes
1 pound angel hair pasta, cooked per package instructions and drained
Salt and pepper to taste
4 tablespoons capers, drained
½ cup grated Parmesan cheese
2 to 4 tablespoons fresh (or dried) parsley, for garnish

Heat oil in a large skillet over medium heat. Add garlic and tomatoes; cook until fragrant and tender. Add cooked pasta and season. Toss to coat and stir in capers. Top with Parmesan and parsley.

This is a simple yet delicious dish. It's one of those meals whose ingredients are always in the cabinet even when you feel like the cupboards are bare. It's ready in minutes and a big bowl of pasta really hits the spot after a long day. Serve with a side salad for a little added green.

This one pan meal is easy, delicious and one of my favorite versions of chili. Did I mention healthy? Kale is one of the healthiest greens for your body and because it's sautéed, all those vitamins stay right in the pan. The jalapeño adds just enough heat to make this dish interesting. Add some crusty bread for dipping.

Kale & White Bean Chili

Yield: 4 servings

1 small onion, chopped
4 garlic cloves, chopped
1 tablespoon seeded, finely chopped jalapeño pepper (optional)
2 tablespoons butter
1 (14-ounce) can vegetable stock
1 (15-ounce) can cannellini beans (white kidney), drained and rinsed
1 (15-ounce) can chickpeas, drained and rinsed
1 teaspoon chili powder
1 teaspoon cumin
1 teaspoon paprika
Salt and pepper to taste
4 cups tightly packed kale, stems removed

In a large skillet or stockpot, sauté onion, garlic and pepper in butter. Add stock, beans and seasonings. Bring to a boil. Cook 10 to 15 minutes to reduce sauce slightly. Remove approximately 1 cup beans, mash and return to sauce to thicken. Add chopped kale, cover and simmer until kale is wilted, 5 to 7 minutes.

Tofu Stir-Fry

Yield: 2 to 4 servings

1 tablespoon sesame oil
½ pound extra-firm tofu, cut into chunks
1 (14.5-ounce) can stir-fry mixed vegetables
2 tablespoons soy sauce
2 cups cooked brown rice
2 scallions, finely chopped

Place sesame oil in a skillet over medium-high heat. Add tofu and fry, tossing to cook on all sides, until brown and heated through, about 10 minutes. Add vegetables and soy sauce; toss to coat. Cook an additional 5 minutes. Serve over rice; garnish with scallions.

You can't beat stir-fry for a quick, one-pan meal. It's veggies and protein all in one and is ready in minutes.

I love a good heart-warming casserole on a cool day. Pop it in the oven and an hour later it comes out hot and bubbly. Because it's so filling, we almost always have leftovers so guess what the kiddos are having for lunch or after-school snack the next day when they get off the bus starving? It's delicious and nutritious which qualifies this dish as a busy mom-approved supper.

Broccoli & Cauliflower Casserole

Yield: 6 to 8 servings

1 head fresh broccoli, chopped
1 head fresh cauliflower, chopped
4 tablespoons butter, softened
3 cups milk, room temperature (not cold)
Salt and pepper to taste
2 cups shredded sharp Cheddar cheese
2 cups shredded mild Cheddar cheese, divided
2 eggs, beaten
1 tablespoon onion powder
10 ounces baby bella mushrooms, sliced
½ cup sour cream
3 tablespoons flour

Preheat oven to 400°. In a bowl, combine all ingredients, using 1 cup mild Cheddar cheese, and toss to coat evenly. Pour into a 9x13-inch greased casserole dish. Cover and bake 30 minutes. Uncover and bake an additional 30 minutes. Top with remaining cheese and bake 5 minutes.

Because I said so. —Every. Mother. Ever.

Y ou glance at your calendar and realize you've committed to the school or church bake sale this weekend. If you are like me, you have absolutely no idea what to make, not to mention all of the other activities already planned. Or how about this scenario? You get a last-minute invite to a weekend barbecue at the neighbors, and you're asked to bring dessert. We've all been in this situation. It's been a long week. You're exhausted, and your weekend is shaping up to be just as busy as your work week. This chapter is full of easy, go-to sweets to make in a pinch. And guess what? They are delicious enough to make even when you have time to plan ahead.

Many of these recipes come from my childhood—recipes from my grandmas, aunts, cousins, and, of course, my mom. I've even included one from my very own Kaden. I'm not really a baker. I mean I can whip up tasty treats in a "jiffy" but it's not really my "jam," puns intended! My mom, however, takes the prize for best baker and dessert maker ever.

These recipes have been researched and tested over many years. Mom was very involved in our community, mainly through the activities of her children. She never said no to a community bake sale fund-raiser whether it was for our church, our schools, or our baseball team. If she wasn't baking for a fund-raiser then she was baking for holidays, company parties, or family gatherings.

Mom made everything from scratch. However, she taught me that just because it's from scratch doesn't necessarily mean it has to be complicated. Let's just face it, who has time for complicated? These recipes are tried-and-true, go-to dessert recipes for the busy mom. Whether you've committed to donating your baked goods for a great cause or you're looking for something to do with the kiddos on a rainy day, the options in this chapter may not be terribly fancy but they are tasty.

F2T Fabulous Tip: Make a dessert with the kiddos to eat with dinner. How many of us have dessert on a weeknight unless it's someone's birthday or a holiday? I usually order it at a restaurant, but I don't generally make dessert at home. A surprise sweet after dinner definitely says, "we're celebrating something special." Maybe you have dessert every night. If so, include the kiddos in the prep and let them serve it to the whole family. It will make them feel as though they are contributing to the meal in an extra-special way.

This is one of our go-to desserts no matter the time of year. It's very light but super flavorful, and I just love citrus in any recipe. The combination of both orange and lemon makes this Jell-O mold extra fragrant and delicious. No matter the event, from graduation parties to the 4th of July, this dessert was always on Mom's table. Thanks Mom!

Mom's Jell-O Mold

Yield: 6 to 8 servings

Lemon Layer:

2 (3.9-ounce) boxes instant lemon pudding
2 cups whole milk
2 (8-ounce) containers Cool Whip

Combine pudding mix with milk. Whisk 2 minutes until thickened. Stir in Cool Whip and chill.

Orange Layer:

4 (3.9-ounce) boxes orange Jell-O
4 cups boiling water
4 cups cold water
3 (15-ounce) cans Mandarin oranges, drained
2 (20-ounce) cans crushed pineapple, drained

Pour Jell-O into a large bowl. Add boiling water and stir until gelatin dissolves (about 2 minutes). Add cold water; mix well. Refrigerate until slightly thin. Add oranges and pineapple; stir until evenly distributed. Return to refrigerator and chill until fully set. Cover generously with lemon topping and serve chilled.

Old-Fashioned Oatmeal Cookies

Yield: 2 to 4 servings

½ cup plus 6 tablespoons butter, softened
¾ cup brown sugar
½ cup sugar
2 eggs
1 teaspoon vanilla extract
1½ cups almond flour
1 teaspoon baking soda
1 teaspoon cinnamon
½ teaspoon salt
3 cups old-fashioned oats
1 cup golden raisins

Preheat oven to 350°. Combine all ingredients. Drop by tablespoonfuls on an ungreased baking sheet. Bake about 25 minutes or until golden brown.

Hands down, this is my son's favorite cookie. He will pick this over any other kind of cookie every single time, even chocolate chip. The smell of this cookie permeating throughout the house is better than any scented candle around. I sold my house its first weekend on the market due to the smell of these little beauties baking in the oven, true story. Well that, and location, location, location. Rhode Island is a lovely state and who doesn't love a house by the water. That's a story for a different book.

Kaden discovered this recipe and thought it was the most fabulous idea ever for kids who don't like to eat healthy. I say sneak the good stuff in wherever you can, especially in chocolate.

Super-Smoothie Brownies

Yield: 8 to 10 servings

1 (18.4-ounce) box brownie mix, plus ingredients to prepare
½ (14.5-ounce) can black beans
½ cup baby kale

Mix brownies per box directions and set aside. Rinse beans. In a food processor (or Nutri Bullet), blend beans, baby kale and 2 tablespoons water into a thick paste. Add to brownie batter and mix thoroughly. Spread in a 9x13-inch greased baking dish and bake per instructions on package.

No-Fail Homemade Cupcakes

Cupcakes:
1 egg
1 cup sugar
½ cup shortening
1 cup sour cream
2 cups flour
1 cup milk
2 teaspoons baking powder
1 teaspoon vanilla extract
½ teaspoon salt

Icing:
2 tablespoons milk
2 cups powdered sugar
½ teaspoon vanilla extract
2 tablespoons butter, softened

Preheat oven to 350°. In a bowl, combine all ingredients and mix thoroughly. Fill cupcake pan, with liners, three-quarters full. Bake 35 to 40 minutes; cool completely before icing. Combine all ingredients for icing. Pour into a zip-close plastic bag. Snip off the corner and pipe generous amount of icing on top of each cupcake. You may add food coloring to your frosting. Divide frosting for different colors.

The smell of these cupcakes baking in the oven takes me right back to my childhood. Back then you could take just about anything into school to share with your class for a birthday party or holiday. These are just as much fun to make and eat at home with the kiddos. Need an excuse? Plan a sleepover. When my son has friends over, they devour everything in the house. I love to have lots of fun options to make the night extra special.

These muffins are yummy, especially served warm with vanilla ice cream. They make a great breakfast option, too, with coffee. It is a terrific way to use up those brown bananas on your countertop. We all have them, believe me.

Chocolate Chip & Banana-Nut Muffins

Yield: 18 to 24 muffins

1 cup mashed overripe bananas
(approximately 3 small)
1 cup semisweet chocolate morsels
1 cup finely chopped walnuts
1 cup sugar
2½ cups flour
3 tablespoons vegetable oil
1 teaspoon salt
1 tablespoon baking powder
¾ cup milk
1 egg
½ cup sour cream

Preheat oven to 350°. Combine all muffin ingredients in a bowl; mix until well blended. Fill cupcake pan, with liners, three-quarters full. Bake 45 minutes or until toothpick inserted in center comes out clean.

Who doesn't love a chocolate chip cookie? I mean, it's the quintessential cookie, in my humble opinion. When we were little, my grandma Storm always had a cookie jar just inside the back door on the counter. I would be so happy when that big glass jar was filled with chocolate chip cookies. They're my favorite! This cookie bar is a little easier for the busy mom because rather than making individual cookies, the batter can be poured into a baking dish to be made all at one time and yes, they are equally delicious.

Chocolate Chip Cookie Bars

Yield: 16 squares

1 cup flour
⅛ cup almond flour
½ teaspoon baking soda
½ teaspoon salt
¼ cup sugar
1 stick butter, softened
½ cup packed light brown sugar
½ teaspoon vanilla extract
1 large egg
1 cup semisweet chocolate morsels
1 cup chopped walnuts

Preheat oven to 375°. In a bowl, combine all ingredients and mix well. Pour into an 8x8-inch ungreased baking dish. Bake 30 minutes or until golden brown. Yield: 16 (1-inch) squares

Pistachio Delight

Crust:
1 cup flour
½ cup finely chopped walnuts
1 stick butter, softened
Dash salt

First Layer:
1 (8-ounce) carton cream cheese, softened
1 cup powdered sugar
2 cups Cool Whip, divided

Second Layer:
2 (3.9-ounce) boxes instant pistachio pudding
3 cups cold milk

Preheat oven to 350°. Mix crust ingredients and press into the bottom of a 9x13-inch pan. Bake 15 minutes; remove to cool. In a bowl, combine cream cheese, powdered sugar and 1 cup Cool Whip; spread over cooled crust. In a separate bowl, whisk ingredients for second layer 2 minutes or until thick. Pour evenly over first layer. Top with remaining Cool Whip and serve chilled.

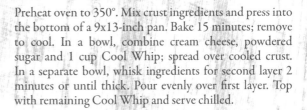

I'm not sure which one of my aunts came up with this recipe. Some say Aunt Nelda. Our family cookbook says Aunt Shirley. Either way, it definitely made it to every party at Grandma Storm's house. It's both refreshing and delicious and is the perfect addition to a summertime barbecue.

This is a fun cookie for the kiddos to make because they can get their hands dirty. Well, that's if you consider your favorite jam on their hands a dirty thing. I say, just lick them clean, kids. This is a great recipe for the holidays and the cookies make a wonderful addition to any Christmas cookie platter.

Shortbread Thumbprints

Yield: 2 dozen

⅔ cup sugar
1 stick butter, softened
½ teaspoon almond extract
2 cups flour
½ cup jam (your preferred flavor)

Preheat oven to 350°. In a bowl, combine all ingredients except jam. Form into 1-inch balls and place on an ungreased cookie sheet. Flatten with thumb, making an indention in each cookie. Fill thumbprint with jam. Bake 25 to 30 minutes until golden brown.

Chocolate Layer Dream

2 (8-ounce) containers whipped
topping, divided
2 (8-ounce) packages cream cheese, softened
2 tablespoons cocoa powder
2 (3.9-ounce) boxes instant chocolate pudding
3 cups cold milk
8 to 10 chocolate cookies
(or 2 brownies), crumbled
16 ounces fresh strawberries, sliced

In a bowl, combine 1½ containers whipped topping along with cream cheese and cocoa powder. Whisk together pudding mix and milk 2 minutes until thick. In a serving bowl (preferably glass), layer cream cheese mixture, cookie crumbles, pudding, then strawberries. Repeat once, then top with reserved whipped topping and remaining strawberries.

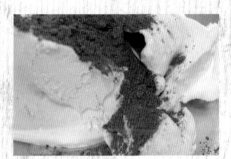

I created this because I love chocolate. I also love a cool, refreshing dessert after a nice meal. You may double this recipe and pile the layers as high as your bowl can accommodate. I don't think anyone will complain about too much chocolate.

Let me start by saying my grandma Kenosky didn't drink alcohol. However, she was very heavy-handed, as they say, with this recipe. If I didn't know better, I'd think she was trying to get us to sleep early on Christmas Eve by serving this for dessert. (I'm teasing of course.) This is one of my favorite desserts any time of the year. It's always a hit because it's unique and delicious.

Grandma's Rum Cake

Yield: 4 to 6 servings

2 (4.6-ounce) boxes cook-and-serve vanilla pudding, plus ingredients to prepare
2 prepared pound cakes, sliced ½-inch thick
3 tablespoons rum (may use rum flavoring)

Prepare pudding per instructions; set aside. In a 9x13-inch casserole dish or pretty glass serving bowl, layer pound cake slices (using about one third) until bottom is covered. Sprinkle with 1 tablespoon rum. Cover with half the pudding mixture. Repeat. Top with remaining pound cake slices and sprinkle with remaining rum. Serve chilled.

Busy Moms' Night In

As a little girl, I was always surrounded by strong, busy women. My grandmothers were two of the hardest working women I knew. Grandma Kenosky ran her own business while Grandma Storm ran a business and farm, both while managing very large households. They cooked breakfast, lunch, and dinner every day, making everything from scratch. Then there's my mom, my role model then and now. She worked full time as a nurse while managing a household and raising two children with my father. She also cooked homemade meals every day, making a point always to put her family first. They did so much for their families while making it look easy, but did they ever get a much needed girls' night?

Our moms' and grandmas' girl time was spent playing pinochle card games with family, at Tupperware parties, at ladies' auxiliary, at church events, or with friends over for pizza on weekend. Their version of girls' night in also usually included a house full of children, so it was anything but relaxing. For the busy moms of today, things aren't much different. We spend a great deal of time managing everyone's schedules, including our own. With the help of kitchen calendars, daily planners, and smartphone alarms, we have become masters of organization. We get our families where they need to be with clean clothes on their backs and food in their bellies. Did I mention that we also get them there on time? Balance is definitely hard to come by and feels like a lot more work to achieve.

With our daily lives so hurried and rushed, it is very hard to think about what we need. Our desires are probably the last thing to cross our minds, a fleeting thought at the end of the day while we plan for the next. On any given night, after everyone has had dinner, my inner monologue ranges from *Does Kaden need a shower?* and *Is the laundry finished?* to *Does Ian have clean shirts?* and *What am I making for dinner tomorrow night?* The train of thoughts seems to go on endlessly with little attention to my needs. As mothers, we often wear many "hats" whether we work outside

or inside the home. Time and again, the "hat" we forget to put on is our own—the one that makes us a human being instead of a human *doing*.

Over the winter, I watched the movie *Bad Moms* one cold afternoon while recipe testing and writing. There's a scene in the movie in which one mom throws an "old-school" party for the PTA, complete with Jell-O shots and countertop dancing. What inspired me was not the crazy party itself but, instead, the representation of every mom group imaginable letting loose and having a good time, guilt free. I'm pretty sure none of their children were starved or neglected as a result, either. For some reason, even letting the thought of doing something for ourselves sneak into our heads triggers guilt because Heaven forbid we're distracted from our daily routines and to-do lists. Stirred by the

APR
13

Girl's Night-In Sips &
Snacks!

Kimberly Ann Storm · Private

movie, I had a bit of an a-ha moment, and now I want moms everywhere to hear the message: Take time for yourself. More importantly, take time to surround yourself with fabulous women that inspire you. Go back, ladies, to that moment in your childhood when spending time with your girlfriends was a priority. It's in that moment, in that place in your mind, where you'll discover what you need as a busy mom—some much-needed girl time.

I became obsessed with the idea of not just telling friends that we should get together soon but actually doing it on a large scale. So how did I pull it off? I created a private event through Facebook and invited my guests one by one. For those friends without social media, I made phone calls to ensure they weren't forgotten. I invited friends from elementary school, college, and beyond. I invited friends who weren't moms because every woman needs a night for herself. I'm truly inspired by other women, so I even invited women I'd only spoken to once, hoping I'd get to know them better. I also encouraged guests to bring a friend just in case anyone was left out or had a friend in need of a girls' night.

Remember, while you're deciding whom to invite, that all your friends have one thing in common—you. You've chosen to surround yourself with friends that are absolutely right for you. You connect with them for a reason, whether it is for a lifetime or a season. Maybe they helped get you through a difficult time, but now you're too busy to see one another. Perhaps you came together for a fundraiser, marathon, or common goal. Regardless, don't be afraid that if you invite friends from kindergarten, they won't mesh with ladies from your child's soccer team. I'm willing to bet that, old or new, the friends you invite will have many of the same qualities. We all have many things in common as women in general, so let that fact alone give you the confidence. I had women tell me that they almost didn't come because they weren't sure if they'd know anyone but ended up walking away with brand-new friends. Be the bridge. Don't let fear hold you back.

As I thought more about the details of my get-together, I figured I could make the evening a little easier on myself by suggesting everyone bring a snack or sip. Think nostalgic potluck dinner with a twist. I also suggested they bring talent, games, stories, or anything else they might want to contribute. I didn't want to put pressure on anyone that had a million other commitments that day or the next. I also didn't want anyone to think they needed to cook or bake for forty to fifty people. All they needed to bring was a little something to share. Above all, I wanted everyone to come, feel comfortable, and enjoy themselves.

Now, I'm not going to lie. Inviting this many women to your home can be intimidating when you're not the best housekeeper in the world. Let's just say that cleaning is not necessarily my forte. For me, cleaning was the most stressful part because I hadn't done a thorough spring cleaning in a very long time. As we were just coming out of a very harsh winter, even the windows had an extra layer of dust, but there's nothing like a party to get some household projects done. I'll give you a tip that would have saved me hours of cleaning: it is really only necessary to clean your kitchen and bathroom. The kitchen and bathroom (and maybe the dining room) are the only rooms anyone will use. Trust me! Everyone loves a kitchen at a party for the obvious reason—food! I didn't realize I could fit more than thirty women into my kitchen until I did it. It's one of the smallest rooms in my house, but no one seemed to care. They're not looking into corners because they're just happy to be out, having a good time with friends.

Though my largest contribution to the evening was the venue, it would be pretty impossible for me to plan a get-together without food. I mean, homemade food is my passion. What I didn't want to do was to put so much pressure on myself that I was too stressed or tired to enjoy the evening's company. Because I asked guests to bring something, I knew there would be plenty of food. I decided, instead, to contribute something fun and trendy—a grazing table. It's very cost effective, quick, and super creative. A grazing table also encourages your friends to circulate into more than one room. And who doesn't love to graze?

To prepare the table, I ran a burlap runner down the center of my dining table and topped it with wax paper. Because both were the same width, it worked beautifully and the wax paper made clearing up a breeze. The room was already decorated for Easter, so I had a little sparkle. A few candles or fairy lights around the room wouldn't go amiss if you'd like to make it extra special. I wouldn't suggest candles on the table because it may interfere with guests serving themselves if they have to reach over an open flame. For tableware, I provided clear plastic plates, toothpicks, and napkins. Easy, right? That's it!

Afterward, I arranged the table with multiple bowls of assorted olives, cheeses, vegetable platters, fruit platters, sliced smoked kielbasa, dips, and salsas. I also placed bunches of grapes, assorted chips, saltines, breads, snack mixes, and assorted nuts directly onto the wax paper to create a very full grazing table. As for drinks, we own a winery, and my husband, Ian, is an incredibly talented winemaker. In addition to wine, I prepared a large beverage dispenser full of vodka, club soda,

ice, sliced lemons, sliced limes, sliced cucumbers, and sliced oranges for a light, refreshing, low-calorie cocktail (1 part vodka to 3 parts club soda, regardless of beverage dispenser size). I also provided water and non-alcoholic beverages for the designated drivers.

Before I knew it, guests were arriving. Greeting each newcomer was like Christmas morning, over and over and over! I mean, truly, I almost forgot whom I had invited until I opened the door each time. Seeing the smiling faces of friends I see every once in a while was so awesome that it made my heart sing. I was happy to know we'd have a full evening of uninterrupted time just to talk, catch up, laugh, drink, and eat. Each of my friends arrived with the most beautiful platters of food they'd created for the evening. What an incredible gift! We had every kind of dessert and finger food imaginable.

Soon, the kitchen countertops brimmed with some of the best food I'd ever tasted. A couple of the ladies even brought lovely note cards and a fun game. Before we knew it, it was 1:30 in the morning, and phones were ringing with husbands wondering if their wives were okay. You see, most of these ladies had commitments the next day and planned to leave a little early, but that didn't happen in every case.

It's hard to articulate how blessed I felt to be surrounded by such an amazing group of women. What's very clear to me now is that spending time with these women is exactly what my soul needed and will need again. If you're wondering what's missing from your life, it's a Moms' Night In. It will refresh your mind, body, and spirit. As busy moms, we must reward ourselves once in a while. You don't need a hard and fast reason to host your get-together. Motherhood is the hardest and most rewarding job you'll ever have, so celebrate! Did you get your children out the door in one piece today, cleaned, groomed, clothed, and fed? Well, there's your reason to celebrate. Even if you've done half of those things, there's reason to celebrate. Let me go a step further by asking, *Did you get out of bed today?* Then that's reason to celebrate and thank God for your blessings.

I have a feeling my Moms' Night In might be the first of many magical nights to come. Maybe I'll host another, or maybe I'll be invited to someone else's home. Either way, I feel like it's just the beginning. It felt incredibly similar to our Farm to Table Experience in our markets because we brought people together who normally wouldn't have had the opportunity to meet. We created magic even though I didn't expect this to be anything more than a night of fun with some amazing women. I certainly didn't expect to write about it since I didn't even cook. Recipes are the focus of this cookbook, so it didn't occur to me beforehand that my Moms' Night In would get a mention. But, as Ian and I reflected on the evening a couple weeks later, we knew it had to

be a part of *Busy Moms and Farm to Table Fabulous* experiences. My hope is that these get-togethers will become an annual trend for moms everywhere. I know it was an experience I needed. We are all amazing, beautiful, selfless, hard-working, incredibly loving busy moms, and we shouldn't forget to make some time for ourselves in our overbooked, overscheduled, overworked, exhausting—yet rewarding—lives. There's no better gift you could give your children than a happy, balanced, fulfilled mom!

Index of Recipes

C

More Great American Books

NEW

My State Notebook Series

$14.95 • 192 pages • 5⅜ x 8¼ • wire-o-bound

Alabama • Georgia • Mississippi

NEW

Kids in the Kitchen

$18.95 • 256 pages • 7x10
paperbound • full-color

Little Gulf Coast
Seafood Cookbook

$14.95 • 192 pages • 5½x8½
paperbound • full-color

Betty B's Having a Party!
A Holiday Dinner Party Cookbook

$18.95 • 256 pages • 7x9 • paperbound • full-color

Great American Grilling

$21.95 • 288 pages
7x10 • paperbound • full-color

Ultimate Venison Cookbook for Deer Camp

$21.95 • 288 pages
7x10• paperbound • full-color

State Hometown Cookbook Series
A Hometown Taste of America, One State at a Time

EACH: $18.95 • 256 pages • 7x10
paperbound • full-color

Alabama • Georgia • Louisiana • Mississippi
South Carolina • Tennessee • Texas • West Virginia

Church Recipes are the Best

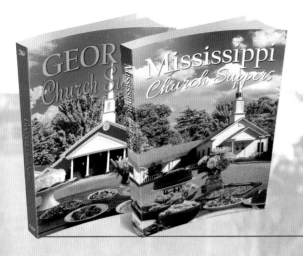

Georgia Church Suppers
$18.95 • 256 pages • 7x10
paperbound • full color

Mississippi Church Suppers
$21.95 • 288 pages • 7x10
paperbound • full color

State Back Road Restaurant Series

Every Road Leads to Delicious Food

EACH: $18.95 • 256 pages • 7x9
paperbound • full-color

Alabama • Kentucky • Louisiana • Missouri
South Carolina • Tennessee • Texas

Eat & Explore Cookbook Series

Discover the USA, Like You've Never Tasted it Before

EACH: $18.95 • 256 pages • 7x9
paperbound • full-color

Arkansas • Illinois • Minnesota • North Carolina
Ohio • Oklahoma • Virginia

If you love Kimberly Storm Ritter's Busy Moms Cookbook.. don't miss her first, best-selling cookbook Farm to Table Fabulous!

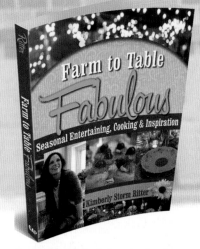

Busy Moms: A Farm to Table Fabulous Cookbook
$18.95 • 256 pages • 7x9
paperbound • full color

Farm to Table Fabulous
$18.95 • 256 pages • 7x9
paperbound • full color

3 Easy Ways to Order

1) Call toll-free **1-888-854-5954** to order by phone or to request a free catalog.

2) Order online at **www.GreatAmericanPublishers.com**

3) Mail a check or money order for the cost of the book(s) plus $5 shipping for the first book and $1 each additional plus a list of the books you want to order along with your name, address, phone and email to:

Great American Publishers
171 Lone Pine Church Road
Lena, MS 39094

Find us on Facebook: www.facebook.com/GreatAmericanPublishers

Join the **We Love 2 Cook Club** and get a 10% discount.
www.GreatAmericanPublishers.com